CLASSIC LOVE PO

Classic
Love Poems

Selected, translated, and adapted
by
John E. Tidball

BISHOPSTON EDITIONS

This anthology first published 2021

Translations and adaptations copyright © 2021
by John E. Tidball

All rights reserved.

ISBN 979 8722815750

CONTENTS

Pierre de Ronsard (1524 – 1585)   Page 14
À Cassandre : Ode to Cassandra
Sonnet pour Hélène : Sonnet for Helen

Nicholas Breton (1542 - 1626)   Page 18
Fair and True

Edmund Spenser (c.1552-1599)   Page 19
Ice and Fire
One day I wrote her name…

Sir Philip Sidney (1554-86)   Page 21
My true love hath my heart…

Michael Drayton (1563-1631)   Page 22
Since there's no help…

William Shakespeare (1564 - 1616)   Page 23
Sonnet 18: *Shall I compare thee to a summer's day?*
Sonnet 116: *Let me not to the marriage of true minds…*
Sonnet 147: *My love is as a fever, longing still...*

Christopher Marlowe (1564 – 1593)   Page 26
The Passionate Shepherd to his Love
Who Ever Loved, That Loved Not at First Sight?

Thomas Campion (c.1567–1619)   Page 28
Amaryllis

Ben Jonson (1572 - 1637)   Page 29
Song to Celia — I : *Come, my Celia, let us prove…*
Song to Celia — II : *Drink to me only with thine eyes…*

John Wilbye (1574 – 1638)   Page 31
Love not me for comely grace…

John Fletcher (1579 - 1625)   Page 32
Take, oh, take those lips away…

Thomas Ford (1580 – 1648)   Page 33
There is a lady sweet and kind…

Robert Herrick (1591-1674)   Page 34
To Virgins, to make much of Time
Sweet Disorder

George Herbert (1593 - 1633)   Page 36
Love

Sir John Suckling (1609 - 1641)   Page 37
I prithee send me back my heart…

Anne Bradstreet (1612 - 1672)   Page 38
To My Dear and Loving Husband

Richard Lovelace (1617 - 1657)   Page 39
Tell me not, Sweet, I am unkind…

John Dryden (1631 - 1700)   Page 40
Hidden Flame

John Wilmot (1647 - 1680)   Page 41
Love and Life

Samuel Johnson (1709 - 1784)   Page 42
Evening Ode
The Winter's Walk
Summer
To Stella

Johann Wolfgang von Goethe (1749-1832)   Page 46
Nähe des Geliebten : Would You Were Here!
Willkommen und Abschied : Welcome and Farewell

William Blake (1757 – 1827)   Page 50
The Garden of Love
My Pretty Rose Tree

Robert Burns (1759-1796)   Page 52
A Red, Red Rose
The Parting Kiss

Amelia Opie (1769 – 1853)   Page 54
Secret Love

Samuel Taylor Coleridge (1772 – 1834)   Page 57
The Presence of Love

Robert Southey (1774 – 1843)   Page 58
Go, Valentine…

Thomas Moore (1779 – 1852)   Page 59
She is far from the land…

George Gordon, Lord Byron (1788-1824)   Page 60
So we'll go no more a-roving…
She walks in beauty…
When we two parted…

Percy Bysshe Shelley (1792-1822)   Page 63
To Jane
Love's Philosophy

John Clare (1793-1864)   Page 65
First Love
How Can I Forget?

John Keats (1795-1821)   Page 67
Bright Star
To Fanny Brawne
You say you love: but with a voice …

Franz von Schober (1796 - 1882)   Page 70
Am Bach im Frühling : By the Brook in Springtime

Heinrich Heine (1797 - 1856)   Page 72
Die Lotosblume : The Lotus Flower
Saphire sind die Augen dein :The Coveted Jewels
Ein Jüngling liebt ein Mädchen : Unrequited Love
Lorelei : Lorelei

Thomas Hood 1799 - 1845)   Page 80
Time of Roses
Ruth

Ludwig Rellstab (1799 - 1860)   Page 82
Ständchen : Serenade

Victor Hugo (1802 – 1885)   Page 84
Demain, dès l'aube… : The Journey

Elizabeth Barrett Browning (1806 – 1861)   Page 86
Sonnet 14 : *If thou must love me, let it be for nought…*
Sonnet 43: *How do I love thee? Let me count the ways.*

Félix Arvers (1806 – 1850)   Page 88
Le Sonnet : The Sonnet

Alfred, Lord Tennyson (1809 - 1892)   Page 90
Break, break, break…
Go not, happy day…
Birds in the high hall garden…
Come into the garden, Maud…

Edgar Allan Poe (1809 - 1849)   Page 96
A Dream Within a Dream
Annabel Lee

Robert Browning (1812 – 1889)   Page 99
Now
Life in a Love

George Eliot (1819 - 1880)   Page 101
Sweet evenings come and go, love...

Charles Kingsley (1819 - 1875)   Page 102
A Farewell
Young and Old

Charles Baudelaire (1821 - 1867)   Page 104
À une passante : To a Passer-By
Le Jet d'eau : The Fountain
L'Invitation au voyage : Invitation to a Journey
Hymne : Hymn
Tout entière : All of Her
Le Portrait : The Portrait
Le Balcon : The Balcony
Le Vin des amants : The Lovers' Wine
La Mort des amants : The Lovers' Death

Matthew Arnold (1822 - 1888)   Page 126
Longing

Stephen Foster (1826 –1864)   Page 127
Beautiful dreamer, wake unto me...
I dream of Jeanie with the light brown hair...

Christina Rossetti (1830 - 1894)   Page 129
Remember
I loved you first...
The First Day
Somewhere or other there must surely be...
Echo

Emily Dickinson (1830 – 1886)   Page 134
A charm invests a face...
For each ecstatic instant...
You left me, sweet, two legacies...
If you were coming in the fall...

William Morris (1834 – 1896)   Page 138
Love is enough: though the World be a-waning…

Alfred Austin (1835 – 1913)   Page 139
Love's Trinity

Henri Cazalis (1840 – 1909)   Page 140
Sérénade florentine : Florentine Serenade
Dans ton cœur dort… : The Antidote

Thomas Hardy (1840 – 1928) Page 144
Neutral Tones
The Voice

Robert Seymour Bridges (1844 – 1930)   Page 146
My delight and thy delight…
So sweet love seemed that April morn…
I will not let thee go…

Paul Verlaine (1844 – 1896)   Page 150
Mon Rêve familier : My Familiar Dream
Chanson d'Automne : Autumn Song

Oscar Wilde (1854 –1900)   Page 154
To My Wife

Edith Nesbitt (1858 - 1924)   Page 155
A Tragedy

A. E. Housman (1859-1936)   Page 156
When the lad for longing sighs…
Oh, when I was in love with you…
When I was one-and-twenty…

Sir Arthur Somervell (1863 –1937)   Page 159
Silent Worship

William Butler Yeats ((1865-1939)   Page 160
When you are old and grey…
Down by the Salley Gardens…

Guillaume Apollinaire (1880 – 1918)   Page 162
Le Pont Mirabeau : The Mirabeau Bridge

Sara Teasdale (1884 – 1933)   Page 164
The Kiss
I am not yours, not lost in you…
Alone

Rupert Brooke (1887 - 1915)   Page 167
Love
Beauty and Beauty

Editor's Note   Page 171

Index of Poets   Page 173

Index of Titles and First Lines   Page 175

THE POEMS

PIERRE DE RONSARD (1524 – 1585)

À Cassandre

Mignonne, allons voir si la rose
Qui ce matin avoit desclose
Sa robe de pourpre au Soleil,
A point perdu ceste vesprée
Les plis de sa robe pourprée,
Et son teint au vostre pareil.

Las! Voyez comme en peu d'espace,
Mignonne, elle a dessus la place
Las! Las! ses beautez laissé cheoir !
Ô vrayment marastre Nature,
Puis qu'une telle fleur ne dure
Que du matin jusques au soir !

Donc, si vous me croyez, mignonne,
Tandis que vostre âge fleuronne
En sa plus verte nouveauté,
Cueillez, cueillez vostre jeunesse :
Comme à ceste fleur la vieillesse
Fera ternir vostre beauté.

PIERRE DE RONSARD (1524 – 1585)

Ode to Cassandra

Come, my sweet Love, to see the rose
That but this morning did unclose
Its robe of crimson to the sun;
Can it have lost, this vesper hour,
The folds of its fair-scented flower,
Pink-blushing like my fairest one?

Alas, see here upon the ground
The crimson petals all around,
So negligently cast aside.
O Nature, whence this wanton duty
To cause a flower to shed its beauty
'Twixt dawn's first light and eventide?

My Love, heed now these words, I pray:
So long as you are blithe and gay
And your sweet youth is in full bloom,
Be sure to cherish every hour,
For careless time, as with this flower,
Will mar your beauty all too soon.

PIERRE DE RONSARD

Sonnet pour Hélène

Quand vous serez bien vieille, au soir à la chandelle,
Assise auprès du feu, dévidant et filant,
Direz, chantant mes vers, en vous esmerveillant,
Ronsard me celebroit du temps que j'estois belle.

Lors vous n'aurez servante oyant telle nouvelle,
Desja sous le labeur à demy sommeillant,
Qui au bruit de Ronsard ne s'aille resveillant,
Benissant vostre nom de louange immortelle.

Je seray sous la terre, et fantaume sans os :
Par les ombres Myrtheux je prendray mon repos.
Vous serez au fouyer une vieille accroupie,

Regrettant mon amour, et vostre fier desdain.
Vivez, si m'en croyez, n'attendez à demain :
Cueillez dés aujourd'huy les roses de la vie.

PIERRE DE RONSARD

Sonnet For Helen

When you are very old, reclining in your chair
Beside the fire, unwinding wool at close of day,
Singing my verses, you in wonderment will say,
Ronsard did honour me when I was young and fair.

There is no servant who, hearing such wonders told,
Though weary from the toilsome duties of the day,
Would not wake from her sleep and rise from where she lay
To celebrate a name that Ronsard once extolled.

And when beneath the earth my mortal soul is laid
In everlasting peace beneath the myrtle's shade,
You'll sit beside the fire, a spinster bowed and bent,

Regretting that you spurned my love so long ago.
Youth is a verdant field where fragrant flowers grow:
Gather your roses now, wait not till life is spent.

NICHOLAS BRETON (1542 - 1626)

Fair and True

Lovely kind, and kindly loving,
Such a mind were worth the moving;
Truly fair, and fairly true —
Where are all these, but in you?

Wisely kind, and kindly wise;
Blessed life, where such love lies!
Wise, and kind, and fair, and true —
Lovely live all these in you.

Sweetly dear, and dearly sweet;
Blessed, where these blessings meet!
Sweet, fair, wise, kind, blessed, true -
Blessed be all these in you!

EDMUND SPENSER (c.1552-1599)

Ice and Fire

My love is like to ice, and I to fire:
How comes it then that this her cold so great
Is not dissolved through my so hot desire,
But harder grows the more I her entreat?
Or how comes it that my exceeding heat
Is not allayed by her heart-frozen cold,
But that I burn much more in boiling sweat,
And feel my flames augmented manifold?
What more miraculous thing may be told,
That fire, which all things melts, should harden ice,
And ice, which is congeal'd with senseless cold,
Should kindle fire by wonderful device?
Such is the power of love in gentle mind,
That it can alter all the course of kind.

EDMUND SPENSER

One day I wrote her name...

One day I wrote her name upon the strand,
But came the waves and washed it away:
Again I wrote it with a second hand,
But came the tide and made my pains his prey.
"Vain man," said she, "that dost in vain essay
A mortal thing so to immortalize;
For I myself shall like to this decay,
And eke my name be wiped out likewise."
"Not so," quoth I; "let baser things devise
To lie in dust, but you shall live by fame;
My verse your virtues rare shall eternize,
And in the heavens write your glorious name:
Where, whenas Death shall all the world subdue,
Our love shall live, and later life renew."

SIR PHILIP SIDNEY (1554-86)

My true love hath my heart....

My true love hath my heart, and I have his,
By just exchange one for the other given:
I hold his dear, and mine he cannot miss;
There never was a bargain better driven.
His heart in me keeps me and him in one;
My heart in him his thoughts and senses guides:
He loves my heart, for once it was his own;
I cherish his because in me it bides.
His heart his wound received from my sight;
My heart was wounded with his wounded heart;
For as from me on him his hurt did light,
So still, methought, in me his hurt did smart:
Both equal hurt, in this change sought our bliss,
My true love hath my heart, and I have his.

MICHAEL DRAYTON (1563-1631)

Since there's no help....

Since there's no help, come let us kiss and part;
Nay, I have done, you get no more of me,
And I am glad, yea glad with all my heart
That thus so cleanly I myself can free;
Shake hands forever, cancel all our vows,
And when we meet at any time again,
Be it not seen in either of our brows
That we one jot of former love retain.
Now at the last gasp of Love's latest breath,
When, his pulse failing, Passion speechless lies,
When Faith is kneeling by his bed of death,
And Innocence is closing up his eyes,
Now if thou wouldst, when all have given him over,
From death to life thou mightst him yet recover.

WILLIAM SHAKESPEARE (1564 - 1616)

Sonnet 18

Shall I compare thee to a summer's day?
Thou art more lovely and more temperate.
Rough winds do shake the darling buds of May,
And summer's lease hath all too short a date.
Sometime too hot the eye of heaven shines,
And often is his gold complexion dimmed;
And every fair from fair sometime declines,
By chance, or nature's changing course, untrimmed;
But thy eternal summer shall not fade,
Nor lose possession of that fair thou ow'st,
Nor shall death brag thou wand'rest in his shade,
When in eternal lines to Time thou grow'st.
So long as men can breathe, or eyes can see,
So long lives this, and this gives life to thee.

WILLIAM SHAKESPEARE

Sonnet 116

Let me not to the marriage of true minds
Admit impediments. Love is not love
Which alters when it alteration finds,
Or bends with the remover to remove.
O no! it is an ever-fixèd mark
That looks on tempests and is never shaken;
It is the star to every wand'ring bark,
Whose worth's unknown, although his height be taken.
Love's not Time's fool, though rosy lips and cheeks
Within his bending sickle's compass come;
Love alters not with his brief hours and weeks,
But bears it out e'en to the edge of doom.
If this be error and upon me proved,
I never writ, nor no man ever loved.

WILLIAM SHAKESPEARE

Sonnet 147

My love is as a fever, longing still
For that which longer nurseth the disease,
Feeding on that which doth preserve the ill,
Th' uncertain sickly appetite to please.
My reason, the physician to my love,
Angry that his prescriptions are not kept,
Hath left me, and I desperate now approve
Desire is death, which physic did except.
Past cure I am, now reason is past care,
And frantic-mad with evermore unrest;
My thoughts and my discourse as madmen's are,
At random from the truth vainly expressed:
For I have sworn thee fair, and thought thee bright,
Who art as black as hell, as dark as night.

CHRISTOPHER MARLOWE (1564 – 1593)

The Passionate Shepherd to his Love

Come live with me, and be my love,
And we will all the pleasures prove,
That hills and valleys, dales and fields,
And all the craggy mountain yields.

There we will sit upon the rocks,
And see the shepherds feed their flocks
By shallow rivers, to whose falls
Melodious birds sing madrigals.

And I will make thee beds of roses,
With a thousand fragrant posies,
A cap of flowers and a kirtle
Embroidered all with leaves of myrtle;

A gown made of the finest wool,
Which from our pretty lambs we pull;
Fair lined slippers for the cold,
With buckles of the purest gold;

A belt of straw and ivy buds,
With coral clasps and amber studs;
And if these pleasures may thee move,
Come live with me, and be my love.

Thy silver dishes for thy meat
As precious as the gods do eat,
Shall on an ivory table be
Prepared each day for thee and me.

The shepherd swains shall dance and sing
For thy delight each May-morning:
If these delights thy mind may move,
Then live with me, and be my love.

CHRISTOPHER MARLOWE

Who Ever Loved, That Loved Not at First Sight?

It lies not in our power to love or hate,
For will in us is overruled by fate.
When two are stripped, long ere the course begin,
We wish that one should love, the other win;
And one especially do we affect
Of two gold ingots, like in each respect:
The reason no man knows, let it suffice,
What we behold is censured by our eyes.
Where both deliberate, the love is slight:
Who ever loved, that loved not at first sight?

THOMAS CAMPION (c.1567–1619)

Amaryllis

I care not for these ladies that must be wooed and prayed;
Give me kind Amaryllis, the wanton country maid.
Nature Art disdaineth; her beauty is her own,
Who when we court and kiss, she cries: forsooth, let go!
But when we come where comfort is, she never will say no.

If I love Amaryllis, she gives me fruit and flowers;
But if we love these ladies, we must give golden showers.
Give them gold that sell love, give me the nut-brown lass,
Who when we court and kiss, she cries: forsooth, let go!
But when we come where comfort is, she never will say no.

These ladies must have pillows and beds by strangers wrought.
Give me a bower of willows, of moss and leaves unbought,
And fresh Amaryllis with milk and honey fed,
Who when we court and kiss, she cries: forsooth, let go!
But when we come where comfort is, she never will say no.

BEN JONSON (1572 - 1637)

Song to Celia – I

Come, my Celia, let us prove
While we may the sports of love;
Time will not be ours forever,
He at length our good will sever.
Spend not then his gifts in vain;
Suns that set may rise again,
But if once we lose this light,
'Tis with us perpetual night.
Why should we defer our joys?
Fame and rumour are but toys
Cannot we delude the eyes
Of a few poor household spies?
Or his easier ears beguile,
So removed by our wile?
'Tis no sin love's fruits to steal;
But the sweet theft to reveal,
To be taken, to be seen,
These have crimes accounted been.

BEN JONSON

Song to Celia – II

Drink to me only with thine eyes,
And I will pledge with mine;
Or leave a kiss within the cup,
And I'll not ask for wine.
The thirst that from the soul doth rise
Doth ask a drink divine;
But might I of Jove's nectar sip,
I would not change for thine.

I sent thee late a rosy wreath,
Not so much honouring thee,
As giving it a hope that there
It would not withered be.
But thou thereon didst only breathe
And send'st it back to me:
Since when it grows, and smells, I swear,
Not of itself, but thee.

JOHN WILBYE (1574 – 1638)

Love not me for comely grace…

Love not me for comely grace,
For my pleasing eye or face,
Nor for any outward part:
No, nor for a constant heart!
For these may fail or turn to ill:
Should thou and I sever.

Keep, therefore, a true woman's eye,
And love me still, but know not why!
So hast thou the same reason still
To dote upon me ever.

JOHN FLETCHER (1579–1625)

Take, oh, take those lips away…

Take, oh, take those lips away
That so sweetly were forsworn
And those eyes, like break of day,
Lights that do mislead the morn;
But my kisses bring again,
Seals of love, though sealed in vain.

Hide, oh, hide those hills of snow,
Which thy frozen bosom bears,
On whose tops the pinks that grow
Are of those that April wears;
But first set my poor heart free,
Bound in those icy chains by thee.

THOMAS FORD (1580—1648)

There is a lady sweet and kind...

There is a lady sweet and kind,
Was never face so pleas'd my mind;
I did but see her passing by,
And yet I love her till I die.

Her gesture, motion, and her smiles,
Her wit, her voice, my heart beguiles,
Beguiles my heart, I know not why,
And yet I love her till I die.

Her free behaviour, winning looks,
Will make a lawyer burn his books;
I touch'd her not, alas! not I,
And yet I love her till I die.

Had I her fast betwixt mine arms,
Judge you that think such sports were harms,
Were't any harm? no, no, fie, fie,
For I will love her till I die.

Should I remain confinèd there
So long as Phoebus in his sphere,
I to request, she to deny,
Yet would I love her till I die.

Cupid is wingèd and doth range
Her country, so my love doth change:
But change she earth, or change she sky,
Yet will I love her till I die.

ROBERT HERRICK (1591-1674)

To Virgins, To Make Much of Time

Gather ye rose-buds while ye may,
Old Time is still a flying:
And this same flower that smiles today,
Tomorrow will be dying.

The glorious lamp of heaven, the sun,
The higher he's a getting;
The sooner will his race be run,
And nearer he's to setting.

That age is best, which is the first,
When youth and blood are warmer;
But being spent, the worse, and worst
Times, still succeed the former.

Then be not coy, but use your time;
And while ye may, go marry:
For having lost but once your prime,
You may forever tarry.

ROBERT HERRICK (1591 – 1674)

Sweet Disorder

A sweet disorder in the dress
Kindles in clothes a wantonness:
A lawn about the shoulders thrown
Into a fine distraction --
An erring lace, which here and there
Enthrals the crimson stomacher --
A cuff neglectful, and thereby
Ribbands to flow confusedly --
A winning wave, deserving note,
In the tempestuous petticoat --
A careless shoe-string, in whose tie
I see a wild civility --
Do more bewitch me than when art
Is too precise in every part.

GEORGE HERBERT (1593 – 1633)

Love

Love bade me welcome. Yet my soul drew back
Guilty of dust and sin.
But quick-eyed Love, observing me grow slack
From my first entrance in,
Drew nearer to me, sweetly questioning,
If I lacked any thing.

A guest, I answered, worthy to be here:
Love said, You shall be he.
I the unkind, ungrateful? Ah my dear,
I cannot look on thee.
Love took my hand, and smiling did reply,
Who made the eyes but I?

Truth Lord, but I have marred them: let my shame
Go where it doth deserve.
And know you not, says Love, who bore the blame?
My dear, then I will serve.
You must sit down, says Love, and taste my meat:
So I did sit and eat.

SIR JOHN SUCKLING (1609 – 1641)

I prithee send me back my heart…

I prithee send me back my heart,
Since I cannot have thine;
For if from yours you will not part,
Why, then, shouldst thou have mine?

Yet now I think on't, let it lie,
To find it were in vain;
For thou hast a thief in either eye
Would steal it back again.

Why should two hearts in one breast lie,
And yet not lodge together?
O Love! where is thy sympathy,
If thus our breasts thou sever?

But love is such a mystery,
I cannot find it out;
For when I think I'm best resolved,
I then am in most doubt.

Then farewell care, and farewell woe;
I will no longer pine;
For I'll believe I have her heart,
As much as she hath mine.

ANNE BRADSTREET (1612 – 1672)

To My Dear and Loving Husband

If ever two were one, then surely we.
If ever man were lov'd by wife, then thee;
If ever wife was happy in a man,
Compare with me ye women if you can.
I prize thy love more then whole Mines of gold,
Or all the riches that the East doth hold.
My love is such that Rivers cannot quench,
Nor ought but love from thee, give recompence.
Thy love is such I can no way repay,
The heavens reward thee manifold I pray.
Then while we live, in love let's so persever,
That when we live no more, we may live ever.

RICHARD LOVELACE (1617 – 1657)

Tell me not, Sweet, I am unkind…

Tell me not, Sweet, I am unkind
For, from the nunnery
Of thy chaste breast, and quiet mind,
To war and arms I fly.

True, a new mistress now I chase,
The first foe in the field;
And with a stronger faith- embrace
A sword, a horse, a shield.

Yet this unconstancy is such
As you too shall adore;
For, I could not love thee, Dear, so much,
Loved I not honour more.

JOHN DRYDEN (1631 - 1700)

Hidden Flame

Feed a flame within, which so torments me
That it both pains my heart, and yet contains me:
'Tis such a pleasing smart, and I so love it,
That I had rather die than once remove it.

Yet he, for whom I grieve, shall never know it;
My tongue does not betray, nor my eyes show it.
Not a sigh, nor a tear, my pain discloses,
But they fall silently, like dew on roses.

Thus, to prevent my Love from being cruel,
My heart's the sacrifice, as 'tis the fuel;
And while I suffer this to give him quiet,
My faith rewards my love, though he deny it.

On his eyes will I gaze, and there delight me;
While I conceal my love no frown can fright me.
To be more happy I dare not aspire,
Nor can I fall more low, mounting no higher.

JOHN WILMOT (1647 – 1680)

Love and Life

All my past life is mine no more,
The flying hours are gone,
Like transitory dreams given o'er,
Whose images are kept in store
By memory alone.

Whatever is to come is not;
How can it then be mine?
The present moment's all my lot;
And that, as fast as it is got,
Phyllis, is wholly thine.

Then talk not of inconstancy,
False hearts, and broken vows;
If I, by miracle, can be
This live-long minute true to thee,
'Tis all that heaven allows.

SAMUEL JOHNSON (1709 – 1784)

Evening Ode

Evening now from purple wings
Sheds the grateful gifts she brings;
Brilliant drops bedeck the mead,
Cooling breezes shake the reed;
Shake the reed, and curl the stream
Silver'd o'er with Cynthia's beam;
Near the chequer'd, lonely grove,
Hears, and keeps thy secrets, love!
Stella, thither let us stray,
Lightly o'er the dewy way.
Phoebus drives his burning car,
Hence, my lovely Stella, far;
In his stead, the queen of night
Round us pours a lambent light:
Light that seems but just to show
Breasts that beat, and cheeks that glow;
Let us now, in whisper'd joy,
Evening's silent hours employ,
Silent best, and conscious shades,
Please the hearts that love invades,
Other pleasures give them pain,
Lovers all but love disdain.

SAMUEL JOHNSON

The Winter's Walk

Behold, my fair, where'er we rove,
What dreary prospects round us rise,
The naked hill, the leafless grove,
The hoary ground, the frowning skies.

Nor only through the wasted plain,
Stern Winter is thy force confess'd;
Still wider spreads thy horrid reign,
I feel thy power usurp my breast.

Enlivening hope, and fond desire,
Resign the heart to spleen and care;
Scarce frighted love maintains her fire,
And rapture saddens to despair.

In groundless hope, and causeless fear,
Unhappy man! behold thy doom;
Still changing with the changeful year
The slave of sunshine and of gloom.

Tired with vain joys, the false alarms,
With mental and corporeal strife,
Snatch me, my Stella, to thy arms,
And screen me from the ills of life.

SAMUEL JOHNSON

Summer

O Phoebus! down the western sky,
Far hence diffuse thy burning ray,
Thy light to distant worlds supply,
And wake them to the cares of day.

Come, gentle Eve, the friend of care,
Come, Cynthia, lovely queen of night!
Refresh me with a cooling breeze,
And cheer me with a lambent light.

Lay me, where o'er the verdant ground
Her living carpet Nature spreads;
Where the green bower with roses crown'd,
In showers its fragrant foliage spreads.

Improve the peaceful hour with wine,
Let music die along the grove;
Around the bowl let myrtles twine,
And every strain be tuned to love.

Come, Stella, queen of all my heart!
Come, born to fill its vast desires!
Thy looks perpetual joy impart,
Thy voice perpetual love inspires.

Whilst all my wish and thine complete,
By turns we languish and we burn,
Let sighing gales our sights repeat,
Our murmurs - murmuring brooks return.

Let me when Nature calls to rest,
And blushing skies the morn foretell,
Sink on the down of Stella's breast,
And bid the waking world farewell.

SAMUEL JOHNSON

To Stella

Not the soft sighs of vernal gales,
The fragrance of the flow'ry vales,
The murmurs of the crystal rill,
The vocal grove, the verdant hill;
Not all their charms, though all unite,
Can touch my bosom with delight.

Not all the gems on India's shore,
Not all Peru's unbounded store,
Not all the power, nor all the fame,
That heroes, kings, or poets claim;
Nor knowledge, which the learn'd approve;
To form one wish my soul can move.

Yet nature's charms allure my eyes,
And knowledge, wealth, and fame I prize;
Fame, wealth, and knowledge I obtain,
Nor seek I nature's charms in vain;
In lovely Stella all combine;
And, lovely Stella! thou art mine.

JOHANN WOLFGANG VON GOETHE (1749 - 1832)

Nähe des Geliebten

Ich denke dein, wenn mir der Sonne Schimmer
Vom Meere strahlt;
Ich denke dein, wenn sich des Mondes Flimmer
In Quellen malt.

Ich sehe dich, wenn auf dem fernen Wege
Der Staub sich hebt;
In tiefer Nacht, wenn auf dem schmalen Stege
Der Wandrer bebt.

Ich höre dich, wenn dort mit dumpfem Rauschen
Die Welle steigt.
Im stillen Hain da geh ich oft zu lauschen,
Wenn alles schweigt.

Ich bin bei dir, du seist auch noch so ferne.
Du bist mir nah!
Die Sonne sinkt, bald leuchten mir die Sterne.
O wärst du da!

JOHANN WOLFGANG VON GOETHE (1749 - 1832)

Would You Were Here!

I think of you when rays of gold
Caress the sea.
I think of you when silver moonbeams
Kiss the lea.

I see you on the lonely road
At break of day;
At dusk, when on my homeward path
I wend my way.

I hear your voice in woodland
When a gentle breeze
Springs up to send a whisper
Through the silent trees.

You're by my side; though you are far,
Yet you are near!
The sun goes down; stars light my path:
Would you were here!

JOHANN WOLFGANG VON GOETHE

Willkommen und Abschied

Es schlug mein Herz, geschwind zu Pferde!
Es war getan fast eh' gedacht.
Der Abend wiegte schon die Erde,
Und an den Bergen hing die Nacht;
Schon stand im Nebelkleid die Eiche,
Ein aufgetürmter Riese, da,
Wo Finsternis aus dem Gesträuche
Mit hundert schwarzen Augen sah.

Der Mond von einem Wolkenhügel
Sah kläglich aus dem Duft hervor,
Die Winde schwangen leise Flügel,
Umsausten schauerlich mein Ohr;
Die Nacht schuf tausend Ungeheuer,
Doch frisch und fröhlich war mein Mut:
In meinen Adern welches Feuer!
In meinem Herzen welche Glut!

Dich sah ich, und die milde Freude
Floss von dem süßen Blick auf mich;
Ganz war mein Herz an deiner Seite
Und jeder Atemzug für dich.
Ein rosenfarbnes Frühlingswetter
Umgab das liebliche Gesicht,
Und Zärtlichkeit für mich – Ihr Götter!
Ich hofft' es, ich verdient' es nicht!

Doch ach, schon mit der Morgensonne
Verengt der Abschied mir das Herz:
In deinen Küssen welche Wonne!
In deinem Auge welcher Schmerz!
Ich ging, du standst und sahst zur Erden,
Und sahst mir nach mit nassem Blick:
Und doch, welch Glück, geliebt zu werden!
Und lieben, Götter, welch ein Glück!

JOHANN WOLFGANG VON GOETHE

Welcome and Farewell

My heart beat fast: to horse! away!
No sooner thought than it was done;
The evening held earth in its sway,
And night upon the mountains hung.
Shrouded in mist there stood the oak,
A giant of colossal size,
While darkness pierced the undergrowth
With myriad atramentous eyes.

Behind a clouded hill the moon
Endeavoured timidly to peer;
On wings of whispered song the winds
Played eerily about my ear;
Night spawned a thousand monsters there,
Yet blithe in spirit on I pressed:
Within my veins what burning fire!
What glowing ardour in my breast!

I saw you, and such tender joy
Flowed from your sweet gaze to my own;
My heart was wholly at your side,
Each breath I took for you alone.
A gentle shade of vernal rose
Upon your features I observed;
Such tenderness for me — ye gods!
So hoped for yet so undeserved!

But with the morning sun's first light
Adieu's sweet sorrow gripped my heart:
In those last kisses what delight!
In those fair eyes what bitter smart!
I went. Your parting gaze was blurred
By tears your heart could not suppress:
And yet, what joy it is to love!
And to be loved, ye gods, what bliss!

WILLIAM BLAKE (1757 – 1827)

The Garden of Love

I went to the Garden of Love.
And saw what I never had seen:
A Chapel was built in the midst,
Where I used to play on the green.

And the gates of this Chapel were shut,
And "Thou Shalt Not", writ over the door;
So I turn'd to the Garden of Love,
That so many sweet flowers bore,

And I saw it filled with graves,
And tomb-stones where flowers should be:
And Priests in black gowns, were walking their rounds,
And binding with briars, my joys & desires.

WILLIAM BLAKE

My Pretty Rose Tree

A flower was offered to me:
Such a flower as May never bore.
But I said "I've a Pretty Rose-tree",
And I passed the sweet flower o'er.

Then I went to my Pretty Rose-tree:
To tend her by day and by night.
But my Rose turn'd away with jealousy:
And her thorns were my only delight.

ROBERT BURNS (1759-1796)

A Red, Red Rose

O my Luve's like a red, red rose
That's newly sprung in June:
O my Luve's like the melodie
That's sweetly play'd in tune.

As fair art thou, my bonnie lass,
So deep in luve am I:
And I will luve thee still, my dear,
Till a' the seas gang dry:

Till a' the seas gang dry, my dear,
And the rocks melt wi' the sun;
I will luve thee still, my dear,
While the sands o' life shall run.

And fare thee weel, my only Luve!
And fare thee weel a while!
And I will come again, my Luve,
Tho' it were ten thousand mile.

ROBERT BURNS

The Parting Kiss

Humid seal of soft affections,
Tenderest pledge of future bliss,
Dearest tie of young connections,
Love's first snowdrop, virgin kiss!

Speaking silence, dumb confession,
Passion's birth, and infant's play,
Dove-like fondness, chaste concession,
Glowing dawn of future day!

Sorrowing joy, Adieu's last action,
(Lingering lips must now disjoin),
What words can ever speak affection
So thrilling and sincere as thine!

AMELIA OPIE (1769 – 1853)

Secret Love

Not one kind look....one friendly word!
Wilt thou in chilling silence sit;
Nor through the social hour afford
One cheering smile, or beam of wit?

Yet still, absorbed in studious care,
Neglect to waste one look on me;
For then my happy eyes may dare
To gaze and dwell unchecked on thee.

And still in silence sit, nor deign
One gentle precious word to say;
For silent I may then remain,
Nor let my voice my soul betray.

This faltering voice, these conscious eyes,
My throbbing heart too plainly speak:
There timid hopeless passion lies,
And bids it silence keep, and break .

To me how dear this twilight hour,
Cheered by the faggot's varying blaze!
If this be mine, I ask no more
On morn's refulgent light to gaze:

For now, while on HIS glowing cheek
I see the fire's red radiance fall,
The darkest seat I softly seek,
And gaze on HIM , unseen by all.

His folded arms, his studious brow,
His thoughtful eye, unmarked, I see;
Nor could his voice or words bestow
So dear, so true a joy on me.

AMELIA OPIE

But he forgets that I am near....
Fame, future fame, in thought he seeks:
To him ambition's paths appear,
And bright the sun of science breaks.

His heart with ardent hope is filled;
His prospects full of beauty bloom:
But, oh! my heart despair has chilled,
My only prospect is....the tomb!

One only boon from Heaven I claim,
And may it grant the fond desire!
That I may live to hear his fame,
And in that throb of joy expire .

Oft hast thou marked my chilling eye,
And mourned my cold reserve to see,
Resolved the fickle friend to fly,
Who seemed unjust to worth and thee:

While I, o'erjoyed, thy anger saw....
Blest proof I had not tried in vain
To give imperious passion law,
And hide my bosom's conscious pain.

But when night's sheltering darkness came,
And none the conscious wretch could view,
How fiercely burned the smothered flame!
How deep was every sigh I drew!

Yet still to thee I'll clothe my brow
In all that jealous pride requires;
My look the type of Ætna's snow....
My heart, of Ætna's secret fires.

AMELIA OPIE

One little moment, short as blest,
Compassion Love's soft semblance wore;
My meagre form he fondly pressed,
And on his beating bosom bore.

His frame with strong emotion shook,
And kindness tuned each faltering word;
While I, surprised, with anxious look
The meaning of his glance explored.

But soon my too experienced heart
Read nought but generous pity there;
I felt presumptuous hope depart,
And all again was dark despair.

Yet still, in memory still, my heart
Lives o'er that fleeting bliss again;
I feel his glance, his touch, impart
Emotion through each bursting vein.

And "Once ," I cry, "those eyes so sweet
On me with fondness deigned to shine;
For once I felt his bosom beat
Against the conscious throbs of mine!"

Nor shall the dear remembrance die
While aught of life to me is given;
But soothe my last convulsive sigh,
And be, till then, my joy....my heaven!

SAMUEL TAYLOR COLERIDGE (1772 – 1834)

The Presence of Love

And in Life's noisiest hour,
There whispers still the ceaseless Love of Thee,
The heart's Self-solace and soliloquy.

You mould my Hopes, you fashion me within;
And to the leading Love-throb in the Heart
Thro' all my Being, thro' my pulse's beat;
You lie in all my many Thoughts, like Light,
Like the fair light of Dawn, or summer Eve
On rippling Stream, or cloud-reflecting Lake.

And looking to the Heaven, that bends above you,
How oft! I bless the Lot that made me love you.

ROBERT SOUTHEY (1774 – 1843)

Go, Valentine

Go, Valentine, and tell that lovely maid
Whom fancy still will portray to my sight,
How here I linger in this sullen shade,
This dreary gloom of dull monastic night;
Say, that every joy of life remote
At evening's closing hour I quit the throng,
Listening in solitude the ring-dome's note,
Who pours like me her solitary song;
Say, that of her absence calls the sorrowing sigh;
Say, that of all her charms I love to speak,
In fancy feel the magic of her eye,
In fancy view the smile illume her cheek,
Court the lone hour when silence stills the grove,
And heave the sigh of memory and of love.

THOMAS MOORE (1779 – 1852)

She is far from the land…

She is far from the land, where her young hero sleeps,
And lovers are round her, sighing;
But coldly she turns from their gaze, and weeps,
For her heart in his grave is lying!
She sings the wild song of her dear native plains,
Every note which he lov'd awaking
Ah! little they think, who delight in her strains,
How the heart of the Minstrel is breaking!

He had lov'd for his love, for his country he died,
They were all that to life had entwin'd him,
Nor soon shall the tears of his country be dried,
Nor long will his love stay behind him.

Oh! make her a grave, where the sun-beams rest,
When they promise a glorious morrow;
They'll shine o'er her sleep, like a smile from the West,
From her own lov'd Island of sorrow!

GEORGE GORDON, LORD BYRON (1788-1824)

So we'll go no more a-roving...

So, we'll go no more a-roving
So late into the night,
Though the heart be still as loving
And the moon be still as bright.

For the sword outwears its sheath
And the soul wears out the breast
And a heart must pause to breathe
And love itself have rest.

Though the night was made for loving
And the day returns too soon,
Yet, we'll go no more a-roving
By the light of the moon.

LORD BYRON

She walks in beauty…

She walks in beauty, like the night
Of cloudless climes and starry skies;
And all that's best of dark and bright
Meet in her aspect and her eyes:
Thus mellowed to that tender light
Which heaven to gaudy day denies.

One shade the more, one ray the less,
Had half impaired the nameless grace
Which waves in every raven tress,
Or softly lightens o'er her face;
Where thoughts serenely sweet express
How pure, how dear their dwelling place.

And on that cheek, and o'er that brow,
So soft, so calm, yet eloquent,
The smiles that win, the tints that glow,
But tell of days in goodness spent,
A mind at peace with all below,
A heart whose love is innocent!

LORD BYRON

When we two parted…

When we two parted
In silence and tears,
Half broken-hearted,
To sever for years,
Pale grew thy cheek and cold,
Colder thy kiss;
Truly that hour foretold
Sorrow to this.

The dew of the morning
Sank chill on my brow
It felt like the warning
Of what I feel now.
Thy vows are all broken,
And light is thy fame:
I hear thy name spoken,
And share in its shame.

They name thee before me,
A knell to mine ear;
A shudder comes o'er me
Why wert thou so dear?
They know not I knew thee,
Who knew thee too well:
Long, long shall I rue thee
Too deeply to tell.

In secret we met
In silence I grieve
That thy heart could forget,
Thy spirit deceive.

If I should meet thee
After long years,
How should I greet thee?
With silence and tears.

PERCY BYSSHE SHELLEY (1792 – 1822)

To Jane

The keen stars were twinkling,
And the fair moon was rising among them,
Dear Jane.
The guitar was tinkling,
But the notes were not sweet till you sung them
Again.
As the moon's soft splendour
O'er the faint cold starlight of Heaven
Is thrown,
So your voice most tender
To the strings without soul had then given
Its own.

The stars will awaken,
Though the moon sleep a full hour later
To-night;
No leaf will be shaken
Whilst the dews of your melody scatter
Delight.

Though the sound overpowers,
Sing again, with your dear voice revealing
A tone
Of some world far from ours,
Where music and moonlight and feeling
Are one.

PERCY BYSSHE SHELLEY

Love's Philosophy

The fountains mingle with the river
And the rivers with the ocean,
The winds of heaven mix for ever
With a sweet emotion;
Nothing in the world is single;
All things by a law divine
In one spirit meet and mingle.
Why not I with thine? —

See the mountains kiss high heaven
And the waves clasp one another;
No sister-flower would be forgiven
If it disdained its brother;
And the sunlight clasps the earth
And the moonbeams kiss the sea:
What is all this sweet work worth
If thou kiss not me?

MUSIC, when soft voices die,
Vibrates in the memory;
Odours, when sweet violets sicken,
Live within the sense they quicken.

Rose leaves, when the rose is dead,
Are heap'd for the beloved's bed;
And so thy thoughts, when thou art gone,
Love itself shall slumber on.

JOHN CLARE (1793-1864)

First Love

I ne'er was struck before that hour
With love so sudden and so sweet,
Her face it bloomed like a sweet flower
And stole my heart away complete.
My face turned pale as deadly pale,
My legs refused to walk away,
And when she looked, what could I ail?
My life and all seemed turned to clay.

And then my blood rushed to my face
And took my eyesight quite away,
The trees and bushes round the place
Seemed midnight at noonday.
I could not see a single thing,
Words from my eyes did start—
They spoke as chords do from the string,
And blood burnt round my heart.

Are flowers the winter's choice?
Is love's bed always snow?
She seemed to hear my silent voice,
Not love's appeals to know.
I never saw so sweet a face
As that I stood before.
My heart has left its dwelling-place
And can return no more.

JOHN CLARE

How Can I Forget?

That farewell voice of love is never heard again
Yet I remember it and think on it with pain
I see the place she spoke when passing by
The flowers were blooming as her form drew nigh
That voice is gone with every pleasing tone
Loved but one moment and the next alone
Farewell the winds repeated as she went
Walking in silence through the grassy bent
The wild flowers they ne'er look'd so sweet before
Bowed in far[e] wells to her they'll see no more
In this same spot the wild flowers bloom the same
In scent and hue and shape aye even name
Twas here she said farewell and no one yet
Has so sweet spoken—How can I forget?

JOHN KEATS (1795 – 1821)

Bright Star

Bright star, would I were stedfast as thou art--
Not in lone splendour hung aloft the night
And watching, with eternal lids apart,
Like nature's patient, sleepless Eremite,
The moving waters at their priestlike task
Of pure ablution round earth's human shores,
Or gazing on the new soft-fallen mask
Of snow upon the mountains and the moors
No--yet still stedfast, still unchangeable,
Pillow'd upon my fair love's ripening breast,
To feel for ever its soft fall and swell,
Awake for ever in a sweet unrest,
Still, still to hear her tender-taken breath,
And so live ever — or else swoon to death.

JOHN KEATS

To Fanny Brawne

I cry your mercy – pity – love! – aye, love!
Merciful love that tantalizes not,
One-thoughted, never-wandering, guileless love,
Unmasked, and being seen -without a blot!
O! let me have thee whole, -all -all -be mine!
That shape, that fairness, that sweet minor zest
Of love, your kiss, -those hands, those eyes divine,
That warm, white, lucent, million-pleasured breast,
Yourself -your soul -in pity give me all,
Withhold no atom's atom or I die,
Or living on, perhaps, your wretched thrall,
Forget, in the mist of idle misery,
Life's purposes, -the palate of my mind
Losing its gust, and my ambition blind!

JOHN KEATS

You say you love: but with a voice …

You say you love; but with a voice
Chaster than a nun's, who singeth
The soft vespers to herself
While the chime-bell ringeth—
O love me truly!

You say you love; but with a smile
Cold as sunrise in September,
As you were Saint Cupid's nun,
And kept his weeks of Ember—
O love me truly!

You say you love; but then your lips
Coral tinted teach no blisses,
More than coral in the sea—
They never pout for kisses—
O love me truly!

You say you love; but then your hand
No soft squeeze for squeeze returneth;
It is like a statue's, dead,—
While mine for passion burneth—
O love me truly!

O breathe a word or two of fire!
Smile, as if those words should burn me,
Squeeze as lovers should—O kiss
And in thy heart inurn me—
O love me truly!

FRANZ VON SCHOBER (1796 - 1882)

Am Bach im Frühling

Du brachst sie nun, die kalte Rinde,
Und rieselst froh und frei dahin.
Die Lüfte wehen wieder linde,
Und Moos und Gras wird neu und grün.

Allein, mit traurigem Gemüte
Tret' ich wie sonst zu deiner Flut.
Der Erde allgemeine Blüte
Kommt meinem Herzen nicht zu gut.

Hier treiben immer gleiche Winde,
Kein Hoffen kommt in meinen Sinn,
Als daß ich hier ein Blümchen finde:
Blau, wie sie der Erinn'rung blühn.

FRANZ VON SCHOBER (1796 - 1882)

By the Brook in Springtime

The brook has shed its icy crust
And blithely flows the vernal stream;
The zephyr breezes waft anew
And moss and grass are fresh and green.

Alone, in sombre mood, I walk
Beside the babbling brook again;
Yet all the beauties of the earth
Do nothing to assuage my pain.

Cold winds now blow within my soul;
All hope has faded from my mind;
E'en though I find a little flower,
Blue, like the ones my memories find.

HEINRICH HEINE (1797 - 1856)

Die Lotosblume

Die Lotosblume ängstigt
Sich vor der Sonne Pracht,
Und mit gesenktem Haupte
Erwartet sie träumend die Nacht.

Der Mond, der ist ihr Buhle
Er weckt sie mit seinem Licht,
Und ihm entschleiert sie freundlich
Ihr frommes Blumengesicht.

Sie blüht und glüht und leuchtet
Und starret stumm in die Höh';
Sie duftet und weinet und zittert
Vor Liebe und Liebesweh.

HEINRICH HEINE (1797 - 1856)

The Lotus Flower

The lotus flower is anxious
Beneath the bright sun's light;
Her head inclined in slumber,
She waits to greet the night.

The moon is her companion,
He wakes her with his rays,
And she unveils her flower-face
Devoutly to his gaze.

She blooms, and glows, and fervently
Looks to the sky above,
Fragrantly, tearfully trembling
With the joy and the sorrow of love.

ll

HEINRICH HEINE

Saphire sind die Augen dein...

Saphire sind die Augen dein,
Die lieblichen, die süßen.
O, dreimal glücklich ist der Mann,
Den sie mit Liebe grüßen.

Dein Herz, es ist ein Diamant,
Der edle Lichter sprühet.
O, dreimal glücklich ist der Mann,
Für den es liebend glühet.

Rubinen sind die Lippen dein,
Man kann nicht schönre sehen.
O, dreimal glücklich ist der Mann,
Dem Liebe sie gestehen.

O, kennt ich nur den glücklichen Mann,
O, daß ich ihn nur fände,
So recht allein im grünen Wald --
Sein Glück hätt' bald ein Ende.

HEINRICH HEINE

The Coveted Jewels

Your eyes are like two sapphires,
So blue, so pure, so sweet!
And three times lucky is the man
Whom they with ardour greet!

Your heart is like a diamond,
With such translucent light
That three times lucky is the man
 On whom it shines tonight!

Your lips are like fine rubies,
Whose colour is so rare
That three times lucky is the man
Who kissed those lips so fair!

If ever I should find that man,
That thrice audacious lover,
Deep in a lonely forest glade,
His luck would soon be over!

HEINRICH HEINE

Ein Jüngling liebt ein Mädchen...

Ein Jüngling liebt ein Mädchen,
Die hat einen andern erwählt;
Der andre liebt eine andre,
Und hat sich mit dieser vermählt.

Das Mädchen heiratet aus Ärger
Den ersten besten Mann,
Der ihr in den Weg gelaufen;
Der Jüngling ist übel dran.

Es ist eine alte Geschichte,
Doch bleibt sie immer neu;
Und wem sie just passieret,
Dem bricht das Herz entzwei.

HEINRICH HEINE

Unrequited Love

A young lad loves a maiden
Who would another wed;
The other loves another
And marries her instead.

The maiden weds in anger
The first and best young buck
Who comes her way thereafter;
The young lad rues his luck.

It is an age-old story,
Yet one that's ever new;
And every time it happens
A heart is rent in two.

HEINRICH HEINE

Lorelei

Ich weiß nicht, was soll es bedeuten
Daß ich so traurig bin;
Ein Märchen aus alten Zeiten
Das kommt mir nicht aus dem Sinn.

Die Luft ist kühl und es dunkelt,
Und ruhig fließt der Rhein;
Der Gipfel des Berges funkelt
Im Abendsonnenschein.

Die schönste Jungfrau sitzet
Dort oben wunderbar,
Ihr goldnes Geschmeide blitzet
Sie kämmt ihr goldenes Haar.

Sie kämmt es mit goldenem Kamme
Und singt ein Lied dabei;
Das hat eine wundersame
Gewaltige Melodei.

Den Schiffer im kleinen Schiffe
ergreift es mit wildem Weh,
Er schaut nicht die Felsenriffe,
Er schaut nur hinauf in die Höh.

Ich glaube, die Wellen verschlingen
Am Ende Schiffer und Kahn;
Und das hat mit ihrem Singen
Die Lorelei getan.

HEINRICH HEINE

Lorelei

I know not why my mind is by
Such sombre thoughts beset;
A haunting tale from long ago
That I cannot forget.

The Rhine is calm as evening's shadows
Lengthen from the West;
The dying embers of the sun
Ignite the clifftop crest.

High on a rugged precipice
There sits a maiden fair;
Her golden jewels glisten
As she combs her golden hair.

She combs it with a golden comb
And sings a song withal,
A strangely lilting melody
That holds men in its thrall.

The boatman, in his fragile craft,
Entranced by thoughts of love,
Is heedless of the jutting rock –
He can but gaze above.

Methinks the waves will swallow up
Both man and boat ere long,
For surely has the Lorelei
Bewitched him with her song.

THOMAS HOOD (1799 - 1845)

Time of Roses

It was not in the Winter
Our loving lot was cast;
It was the time of roses—
We pluck'd them as we pass'd!

That churlish season never frown'd
On early lovers yet:
O no—the world was newly crown'd
With flowers when first we met!

'Twas twilight, and I bade you go,
But still you held me fast;
It was the time of roses—
We pluck'd them as we pass'd!

THOMAS HOOD

Ruth

She stood breast high amid the corn,
Clasped by the golden light of morn,
Like the sweetheart of the sun,
Who many a glowing kiss had won.

On her cheek an autumn flush,
Deeply ripened; such a blush
In the midst of brown was born,
Like red poppies grown with corn.

Round her eyes her tresses fell,
Which were blackest none could tell,
But long lashes veiled a light,
That had else been all too bright.

And her hat, with shady brim,
Made her tressy forehead dim;
Thus she stood amid the stooks,
Praising God with sweetest looks:

Sure, I said, heaven did not mean,
Where I reap thou shouldst but glean,
Lay thy sheaf adown and come,
Share my harvest and my home.

LUDWIG RELLSTAB (1799 - 1860)

Ständchen

Leise flehen meine Lieder
Durch die Nacht zu dir;
In den stillen Hain hernieder,
Liebchen, komm zu mir!

Flüsternd schlanke Wipfel rauschen
In des Mondes Licht;
Des Verräters feindlich Lauschen
Fürchte, Holde, nicht.

Hörst die Nachtigallen schlagen?
Ach! sie flehen dich,
Mit der Töne süßen Klagen
Flehen sie für mich.

Sie verstehn des Busens Sehnen,
Kennen Liebesschmerz,
Rühren mit den Silbertönen
Jedes weiche Herz.

Laß auch dir die Brust bewegen,
Liebchen, höre mich!
Bebend harr' ich dir entgegen!
Komm, beglücke mich!

LUDWIG RELLSTAB (1799 - 1860)

Serenade

Through the darkness my entreaties
Wing their way to thee.
Down into this silent arbour
Come, my love, to me.

Slender treetops whisper softly
In the moonlit haze;
Lovely maiden, do not fear
The watcher's jealous gaze.

Hear the sound of nightingales
Imploring tenderly,
With their songs of sweet lament
They send my prayers to thee.

They discern the bosom's yearning,
Know a lover's pain,
Touching every tender heart
With silver-sweet refrain.

May love's ardour fill thy breast,
My darling, hear my plea!
Trembling, I await our meeting —
Come, enrapture me!

VICTOR HUGO (1802 – 1885)

Demain, dès l'aube…

Demain, dès l'aube, à l'heure où blanchit la campagne,
Je partirai. Vois-tu, je sais que tu m'attends.
J'irai par la forêt, j'irai par la montagne.
Je ne puis demeurer loin de toi plus longtemps.

Je marcherai les yeux fixés sur mes pensées,
Sans rien voir au dehors, sans entendre aucun bruit,
Seul, inconnu, le dos courbé, les mains croisées,
Triste, et le jour pour moi sera comme la nuit.

Je ne regarderai ni l'or du soir qui tombe,
Ni les voiles au loin descendant vers Harfleur,
Et quand j'arriverai, je mettrai sur ta tombe
Un bouquet de houx vert et de bruyère en fleur.

VICTOR HUGO (1802 – 1885)

The Journey

Tomorrow, when the dawn lights up the countryside,
I shall depart; – I know you're waiting for me too.
I'll traverse wood and field, valley and mountainside.
No longer can I bear to be apart from you.

In silence I shall walk, my ears immune to sound,
My eyes fixed on my thoughts, oblivious to sight,
Alone, unrecognised, back bent toward the ground,
And daylight will to me be like the darkest night.

I shall not pause to gaze on evening's golden grace,
Nor watch the distant sails descending on Harfleur,
And then, when I arrive, upon your grave I'll place
A wreath of holly green and flowering heather there.

ELIZABETH BARRETT BROWNING (1806 –1861)

Sonnet 14

If thou must love me, let it be for nought
Except for love's sake only. Do not say,
"I love her for her smile — her look — her way
Of speaking gently, — for a trick of thought
That falls in well with mine, and certes brought
A sense of pleasant ease on such a day" —
For these things in themselves, Belovèd, may
Be changed, or change for thee — and love, so wrought,
May be unwrought so. Neither love me for
Thine own dear pity's wiping my cheeks dry:
A creature might forget to weep, who bore
Thy comfort long, and lose thy love thereby!
But love me for love's sake, that evermore
Thou mayst love on, through love's eternity.

ELIZABETH BARRETT BROWNING

Sonnet 43

How do I love thee? Let me count the ways.
I love thee to the depth and breadth and height
My soul can reach, when feeling out of sight
For the ends of being and ideal grace.
I love thee to the level of every day's
Most quiet need, by sun and candle-light.
I love thee freely, as men strive for right.
I love thee purely, as they turn from praise.
I love thee with the passion put to use
In my old griefs, and with my childhood's faith.
I love thee with a love I seemed to lose
With my lost saints. I love thee with the breath,
Smiles, tears, of all my life; and, if God choose,
I shall but love thee better after death.

FÉLIX ARVERS (1806 – 1850)

Le Sonnet

Mon âme a son secret; ma vie a sa mystère;
Un amour éternel, en un moment conçu,
Le mal est sans espoir, aussi j'ai dû le taire,
Et celle qui l'a fait n'en a jamais rien su.

Hélas! j'aurai passé près d'elle inaperçu,
Toujours â ses côtés, et pourtant solitaire,
Et j'aurai jusqu'au bout fait mon temps sur la terre
N'osant rien demander, et n'ayant rien reçu.

Pour elle, quoique Dieu l'ait faite douce et tendre,
Elle ira son chemin, distraite et sans entendre
Ce murmure d'amour élevé sur ses pas;

A l'austère devoir pieusement fidèle,
Elle dira, lisant ces vers tout remplis d'elle,
« Quelle est donc cette femme ? » et ne comprendra pas.

FÉLIX ARVERS (1806 – 1850)

The Sonnet

My soul conceals a secret, my life a mystery:
A love born in an instant, ever to remain;
A love devoid of hope, a love that cannot be,
And she whom it concerns knows nothing of my pain.

Alas! She'll never know the longing that I feel.
Forever by her side, yet silent and alone,
I shall throughout my life be destined to conceal
This yearning for a heart I dare not make my own.

And she, whom God has made so gentle, sweet, and dear,
Will tread the path of life, never disposed to hear
That silent sigh of love that follows her always.

Piously devoted to life's austere command,
She'll say, hearing these verses singing in her praise:
"Who can this woman be?" and will not understand.

ALFRED, LORD TENNYSON (1809 - 1892)

Break, break, break ...

Break, break, break,
On thy cold grey stones, O Sea!
And I would that my tongue could utter
The thoughts that arise in me.

O, well for the fisherman's boy,
That he shouts with his sister at play!
O, well for the sailor lad,
That he sings in his boat on the bay!

And the stately ships go on
To their haven under the hill;
But O for the touch of a vanish'd hand,
And the sound of a voice that is still!

Break, break, break
At the foot of thy crags, O Sea!
But the tender grace of a day that is dead
Will never come back to me.

ALFRED, LORD TENNYSON

Go not, happy day…

Go not, happy day
From the shining fields,
Go not, happy day,
Till the maiden yields.
Rosy is the West,
Rosy is the South,
Roses are her cheeks,
And a rose her mouth.

When the happy Yes
Falters from her lips,
Pass and blush the news
Over glowing ships;
Over blowing seas,
Over seas at rest,
Pass the happy news,
Blush it thro' the West;

Till the red man dance
By his red cedar-tree,
And the red man's babe
Leap beyond the sea.

Blush from West to East,
Blush from East to West,
Till the West is East,
Blush it thro' the West.
Rosy is the West,
Rosy is the South,
Roses are her cheeks,
And a rose her mouth.

ALFRED, LORD TENNYSON

Birds in the high hall garden…

Birds in the high hall garden
When twilight was falling,
Maud, Maud, Maud, Maud,
They were crying and calling.

Where was Maud? In our wood;
And I, who else? was with her,
Gathering woodland lilies,
Myriads blow together.

Birds in our wood sang,
 Ringing thro' the valleys,
Maud is here, here, here
In among the lilies.

I kiss'd her slender hand,
She took the kiss sedately;
Maud is not seventeen,
But she is tall and stately.

I know the way she went
Home with her maiden posy,
For her feet have touch'd the meadows
And left the daisies rosy.

ALFRED, LORD TENNYSON

Come into the garden, Maud...

Come into the garden, Maud,
For the black bat, Night, has flown,
Come into the garden, Maud,
I am here at the gate alone;
And the woodbine spices are wafted abroad,
And the musk of the roses blown.

For a breeze of morning moves,
And the planet of Love is on high,
Beginning to faint in the light that she loves
On a bed of daffodil sky,
To faint in the light of the sun she loves,
To faint in his light, and to die.

All night have the roses heard
The flute, violin, bassoon;
All night has the casement jessamine stirr'd
To the dancers dancing in tune:
Till a silence fell with the waking bird,
And a hush with the setting moon.

I said to the lily, "There is but one
With whom she has heart to be gay.
When will the dancers leave her alone?
She is weary of dance and play."
Now half to the setting moon are gone,
And half to the rising day;
Low on the sand and loud on the stone
The last wheel echoes away.

I said to the rose, "The brief night goes
In babble and revel and wine.
O young lordlover, what sighs are those
For one that will never be thine?

ALFRED, LORD TENNYSON

But mine, but mine," so I sware to the rose,
"For ever and ever, mine."

And the soul of the rose went into my blood,
As the music clash'd in the hall;
And long by the garden lake I stood,
For I heard your rivulet fall
From the lake to the meadow and on to the wood,
Our wood, that is dearer than all;

From the meadow your walks have left so sweet
That whenever a March-wind sighs
He sets the jewelprint of your feet
In violets blue as your eyes,
To the woody hollows in which we meet
And the valleys of Paradise.

The slender acacia would not shake
One long milk-bloom on the tree;
The white lake-blossom fell into the lake,
As the pimpernel dozed on the lea;
But the rose was awake all night for your sake,
Knowing your promise to me;
The lilies and roses were all awake,
They sigh'd for the dawn and thee.

Queen rose of the rosebud garden of girls,
Come hither, the dances are done,
 In gloss of satin and glimmer of pearls,
Queen lily and rose in one;
Shine out, little head, sunning over with curls,
To the flowers, and be their sun.

There has fallen a splendid tear
From the passion-flower at the gate.

ALFRED, LORD TENNYSON

She is coming, my dove, my dear;
She is coming, my life, my fate;
The red rose cries, "She is near, she is near;"
And the white rose weeps, "She is late;"
The larkspur listens, "I hear, I hear;"
And the lily whispers, "I wait."

She is coming, my own, my sweet;
Were it ever so airy a tread,
My heart would hear her and beat,
Were it earth in an earthy bed;
My dust would hear her and beat,
Had I lain for a century dead;
Would start and tremble under her feet,
And blossom in purple and red.

EDGAR ALLAN POE (1809 - 1849)

A Dream Within a Dream

Take this kiss upon the brow!
And, in parting from you now,
Thus much let me avow--
You are not wrong, who deem
That my days have been a dream;
Yet if hope has flown away
In a night, or in a day,
In a vision, or in none,
Is it therefore the less gone?
All that we see or seem
Is but a dream within a dream.

I stand amid the roar
Of a surf-tormented shore,
And I hold within my hand
Grains of the golden sand--
How few! yet how they creep
Through my fingers to the deep,
While I weep--while I weep!
O God! can I not grasp
Them with a tighter clasp?
O God! can I not save
One from the pitiless wave?
Is all that we see or seem
But a dream within a dream?

EDGAR ALLAN POE

Annabel Lee

It was many and many a year ago,
In a kingdom by the sea,
That a maiden there lived whom you may know
By the name of Annabel Lee;—
And this maiden she lived with no other thought
Than to love and be loved by me.

She was a child and I was a child,
In this kingdom by the sea,
But we loved with a love that was more than love—
I and my Annabel Lee—
With a love that the winged seraphs of Heaven
Coveted her and me.

And this was the reason that, long ago,
In this kingdom by the sea,
A wind blew out of a cloud by night
Chilling my Annabel Lee;
So that her high-born kinsmen came
And bore her away from me,
To shut her up in a sepulchre
In this kingdom by the sea.

The angels, not half so happy in Heaven,
Went envying her and me:—
Yes! that was the reason (as all men know,
In this kingdom by the sea)
That the wind came out of the cloud, chilling
And killing my Annabel Lee.

But our love it was stronger by far than the love
Of those who were older than we—
Of many far wiser than we—
And neither the angels in Heaven above
Nor the demons down under the sea,

Can ever dissever my soul from the soul
Of the beautiful Annabel Lee: —

For the moon never beams without bringing me dreams
Of the beautiful Annabel Lee;
And the stars never rise but I see the bright eyes
Of the beautiful Annabel Lee;
And so, all the night-tide, I lie down by the side
Of my darling, my darling, my life and my bride
In the sepulchre there by the sea —
In her tomb by the side of the sea.

ROBERT BROWNING (1812 – 1889)

Now

Out of your whole life give but a moment!
All of your life that has gone before,
All to come after it, - so you ignore,
So you make perfect the present, condense,
In a rapture of rage, for perfection's endowment,
Thought and feeling and soul and sense,
Merged in a moment which gives me at last
You around me for once, you beneath me, above me -
Me, sure that, despite of time future, time past,
This tick of life-time's one moment you love me!
How long such suspension may linger? Ah, Sweet,
The moment eternal - just that and no more -
When ecstasy's utmost we clutch at the core,
While cheeks burn, arms open, eyes shut, and lips meet!

ROBERT BROWNING

Life in a Love

Escape me?
Never—
Beloved!
While I am I, and you are you,
So long as the world contains us both,
Me the loving and you the loth,
While the one eludes, must the other pursue.
My life is a fault at last, I fear:
It seems too much like a fate, indeed!
Though I do my best I shall scarce succeed.
But what if I fail of my purpose here?
It is but to keep the nerves at strain,
To dry one's eyes and laugh at a fall,
And, baffled, get up and begin again,—
So the chase takes up one's life, that's all.
While, look but once from your farthest bound
At me so deep in the dust and dark,
No sooner the old hope goes to ground
Than a new one, straight to the self-same mark,
I shape me—
Ever
Removed!

GEORGE ELIOT (1819 - 1880))

"La noche buena se viene,
La noche buena se va,
Y nosotros nos iremos
Y no volveremos mas."
-- Old Villancico.

Sweet evenings come and go, love...

Sweet evenings come and go, love,
They came and went of yore:
This evening of our life, love,
Shall go and come no more.

When we have passed away, love,
All things will keep their name;
But yet no life on earth, love,
With ours will be the same.

The daisies will be there, love,
The stars in heaven will shine:
I shall not feel thy wish, love,
Nor thou my hand in thine.

A better time will come, love,
And better souls be born:
I would not be the best, love,
To leave thee now forlorn.

CHARLES KINGSLEY (1819 - 1875)

A Farewell

I

My fairest child, I have no song to give you;
No lark could pipe to skies so dull and grey:
Yet, ere we part, one lesson I can leave you
For every day.

II

Be good, sweet maid, and let who will be clever;
Do noble things, not dream them, all day long:
And so make life, death, and that vast for-ever
One grand, sweet song.

CHARLES KINGSLEY

Young and Old

When all the world is young, lad,
And all the trees are green;
And every goose a swan, lad,
And every lass a queen;
Then hey for boot and horse, lad,
And round the world away!
Young blood must have its course, lad,
And every dog his day.

When all the world is old, lad,
And all the trees are brown;
And all the sport is stale, lad,
And all the wheels run down;
Creep home, and take your place there,
The spent and maimed among;
God grant you find one face there,
You loved when all was young.

CHARLES BAUDELAIRE (1821 - 1867)

A une Passante

La rue assourdissante autour de moi hurlait.
Longue, mince, en grand deuil, douleur majestueuse,
Une femme passa, d'une main fastueuse
Soulevant, balançant le feston et l'ourlet;

Agile et noble, avec sa jambe de statue.
Moi, je buvais, crispé comme un extravagant,
Dans son œil, ciel livide où germe l'ouragan,
La douceur qui fascine et le plaisir qui tue.

Un éclair... puis la nuit! — Fugitive beauté
Dont le regard m'a fait soudainement renaître,
Ne te verrai-je plus que dans l'éternité?

Ailleurs, bien loin d'ici! trop tard! jamais peut-être!
Car j'ignore où tu fuis, tu ne sais où je vais,
Ô toi que j'eusse aimée, ô toi qui le savais!

CHARLES BAUDELAIRE (1821 – 1867)

To a Passer-By

About me roared the noise and clamour of the town.
A widow, new-bereaved, tall, slender, stately, grand,
Passed by, and with a graceful gesture of her hand,
Lifted the scalloped border of her mourning gown.

Enchanted by her grace, her perfect symmetry,
Delirious, I drank, enraptured yet forlorn,
From her eyes, livid skies where hurricanes are born,
The sweetness that enthrals, the lethal ecstasy.

A lightning flash — then night! — O fugitive beauty,
Whose single passing glance kindled new life in me,
Shall I see you again but in eternity?

Elsewhere, so far from here! too late! *never*, maybe?
For I know not your fate, nor you my destiny,
You whom I might have loved, you knew it, fleetingly!

CHARLES BAUDELAIRE

Le Jet d'eau

Tes beaux yeux sont las, pauvre amante!
Reste longtemps, sans les rouvrir,
Dans cette pose nonchalante
Où t'a surprise le plaisir.
Dans la cour le jet d'eau qui jase,
Et ne se tait ni nuit ni jour,
Entretient doucement l'extase
Où ce soir m'a plongé l'amour.

La gerbe épanouie
En mille fleurs,
Où Phoebé réjouie
Met ses couleurs,
Tombe comme une pluie
De larges pleurs.

Ainsi ton âme qu'incendie
L'éclair brûlant des voluptés
S'élance, rapide et hardie,
Vers les vastes cieux enchantés.
Puis elle s'épanche, mourante,
En un flot de triste langueur,
Qui par une invisible pente
Descend jusqu'au fond de mon cœur.

La gerbe épanouie
En mille fleurs,
Où Phoebé réjouie
Met ses couleurs,
Tombe comme une pluie
De larges pleurs.

CHARLES BAUDELAIRE

The Fountain

Your lovely eyes are tired, poor sweet!
Sleep on in that unstudied guise,
So nonchalantly indiscreet,
Where pleasure took you by surprise.
The fountain burbles endlessly
Out in the courtyard, day and night,
Sustaining the sweet ecstasy
That love accorded me tonight.

There blossoms forth a spray
Of floral spheres,
Where Phoebe's bright display
Gaily appears,
And falls in an array
Of heavy tears.

And thus your ardent soul ignites
In hedonistic ecstasy,
And rushes boldly to the heights
Of the vast sky's infinity,
Until, expiring, losing hope,
In languid dole it falls apart,
Cascading down a hidden slope
Into the haven of my heart.

There blossoms forth a spray
Of floral spheres,
Where Phoebe's bright display
Gaily appears,
And falls in an array
Of heavy tears.

CHARLES BAUDELAIRE

Ô toi, que la nuit rend si belle,
Qu'il m'est doux, penché vers tes seins,
D'écouter la plainte éternelle
Qui sanglote dans les bassins!
Lune, eau sonore, nuit bénie,
Arbres qui frissonnez autour,
Votre pure mélancolie
Est le miroir de mon amour.

La gerbe épanouie
En mille fleurs,
Où Phoebé réjouie
Met ses couleurs,
Tombe comme une pluie
De larges pleurs.

CHARLES BAUDELAIRE

You whom the night doth render fair,
How sweet it is, upon your breast,
To hear, in the ethereal air,
The fountains sobbing without rest!
Moon, rippling water, blessed night,
Leaves whispering in the trees above,
The languor of your sweet delight
Is the reflection of my love.

There blossoms forth a spray
Of floral spheres,
Where Phoebe's bright display
Gaily appears,
And falls in an array
Of heavy tears.

CHARLES BAUDELAIRE

L'Invitation au voyage

Mon enfant, ma sœur,
Songe à la douceur
D'aller là-bas vivre ensemble!
Aimer à loisir,
Aimer et mourir
Au pays qui te ressemble!
Les soleils mouillés
De ces ciels brouillés
Pour mon esprit ont les charmes
Si mystérieux
De tes traîtres yeux,
Brillant à travers leurs larmes.

Là, tout n'est qu'ordre et beauté,
Luxe, calme et volupté.

Des meubles luisants,
Polis par les ans,
Décoreraient notre chambre;
Les plus rares fleurs
Mêlant leurs odeurs
Aux vagues senteurs de l'ambre,
Les riches plafonds,
Les miroirs profonds,
La splendeur orientale,
Tout y parlerait
À l'âme en secret
Sa douce langue natale.

Là, tout n'est qu'ordre et beauté,
Luxe, calme et volupté.

CHARLES BAUDELAIRE

Invitation to a Journey

My sister, my heart,
How sweet to depart
To that faraway haven with you!
To languidly lie,
To love and to die
In a land that resembles you!
The damp suns that rise
In those nebulous skies
Seem to mirror the charm that appears
In the mystic disguise
Of your treacherous eyes,
Glistening through their tears.

There, all is order and beauty,
Luxury, calm and ecstasy.

Furnishings fine,
Embellished by time,
Would decorate our room;
And flowers most rare
Their fragrance would share
With amber's heady perfume,
Mirrors ornate,
And walls with the weight
Of Orient's splendour hung,
All things there would speak
In the secret mystique
Of their gentle native tongue.

There, all is order and beauty,
Luxury, calm, and ecstasy.

CHARLES BAUDELAIRE

Vois sur ces canaux
Dormir ces vaisseaux
Dont l'humeur est vagabonde;
C'est pour assouvir
Ton moindre désir
Qu'ils viennent du bout du monde.
— Les soleils couchants
Revêtent les champs,
Les canaux, la ville entière,
D'hyacinthe et d'or;
Le monde s'endort
Dans une chaude lumière.

Là, tout n'est qu'ordre et beauté,
Luxe, calme et volupté.

CHARLES BAUDELAIRE

See the vessels that brave
The wind and the wave
Rocking gently in their berth;
It is to inspire
Your every desire
That they come from the ends of the earth.
— The sun goes down,
Setting the town,
The meadows and rivers alight
With jacinth and gold;
Our dreams unfold
In a gently warming light.

There, all is order and beauty,
Luxury, calm and ecstasy.

CHARLES BAUDELAIRE

Hymne

À la très chère, à la très belle
Qui remplit mon cœur de clarté,
À l'ange, À l'idole immortelle,
Salut en l'immortalité!

Elle se répand dans ma vie
Comme un air imprégné de sel,
Et dans mon âme inassouvie
Verse le goût de l'éternel.

Sachet toujours frais qui parfume
L'atmosphère d'un cher réduit,
Encensoir oublié qui fume
En secret à travers la nuit,

Comment, amour incorruptible,
T'exprimer avec vérité?
Grain de musc qui gis, invisible,
Au fond de mon éternité!

À la très bonne, à la très belle
Qui fait ma joie et ma santé,
À l'ange, à l'idole immortelle,
Salut en l'immortalité!

CHARLES BAUDELAIRE

Hymn

To her most dear, to her most fair
Who fills my heart with clarity,
To an angel beyond compare,
Greetings in immortality!

She flows into my consciousness
Like a salt breeze's soft caress,
And into my unsated soul
She pours a taste of timelessness.

Ever fresh sachet which perfumes
A cherished place with sweet delight,
Forgotten incense bowl which fumes
In secrecy throughout the night,

How, love that's incorruptible,
Can I describe you truthfully?
A grain of musk, invisible,
Deep in my soul's eternity!

To her most dear, to her most fair,
My joy and my felicity,
To an angel beyond compare,
Greetings in immortality!

CHARLES BAUDELAIRE

Tout entière

Le Démon, dans ma chambre haute
Ce matin est venu me voir,
Et, tâchant à me prendre en faute
Me dit: « Je voudrais bien savoir

Parmi toutes les belles choses
Dont est fait son enchantement,
Parmi les objets noirs ou roses
Qui composent son corps charmant,

Quel est le plus doux. » — Ô mon âme!
Tu répondis à l'Abhorré:
 « Puisqu'en Elle tout est dictame
Rien ne peut être préféré.

Lorsque tout me ravit, j'ignore
Si quelque chose me séduit.
Elle éblouit comme l'Aurore
Et console comme la Nuit;

Et l'harmonie est trop exquise,
Qui gouverne tout son beau corps,
Pour que l'impuissante analyse
En note les nombreux accords.

Ô métamorphose mystique
De tous mes sens fondus en un!
Son haleine fait la musique,
Comme sa voix fait le parfum! »

CHARLES BAUDELAIRE

All of Her

The Devil came to call on me
This morning in my attic room,
And, seeking to befuddle me,
Said: "Tell me, if I may presume,

Among the wonders that compose
The beauty of her form so fair,
Among the objects, black or rose,
That lend her such a charming air,

Which is the sweetest?" — O my Soul!
You did reply to the Abhorred:
"In truth, she is a perfect whole:
Each virtue brings its own reward.

Her every feature gives delight —
What charms me most? I do not know.
She is the solace of the Night,
The radiance of Aurora's glow.

A most exquisite harmony
Pervades the union of her arts,
And no impotent scrutiny
Can separate the diverse parts.

O mystic metamorphosis
Of every sense uniquely blent!
Her breath is music's synthesis,
And her voice gives forth fragrant scent!"

CHARLES BAUDELAIRE

Le Portrait

La Maladie et la Mort font des cendres
De tout le feu qui pour nous flamboya.
De ces grands yeux si fervents et si tendres,
De cette bouche où mon cœur se noya,

De ces baisers puissants comme un dictame,
De ces transports plus vifs que des rayons,
Que reste-t-il? C'est affreux, ô mon âme!
Rien qu'un dessin fort pâle, aux trois crayons,

Qui, comme moi, meurt dans la solitude,
Et que le Temps, injurieux vieillard,
Chaque jour frotte avec son aile rude...

Noir assassin de la Vie et de l'Art,
Tu ne tueras jamais dans ma mémoire
Celle qui fut mon plaisir et ma gloire!

CHARLES BAUDELAIRE

The Portrait

Disease and Death reduce to ash and cinder
Our passion that once burned with ardent fire.
Of those wide eyes so fervent and so tender,
That mouth where my heart drowned in deep desire,

Of those clandestine kisses that we stole,
Those transports more intense than lambent rays,
What now remains? It's awful, O my soul!
Just a three-coloured sketch, a pallid haze,

Which, like me, dies and slowly fades away,
And which harsh Time, malignant patriarch,
Abrades with his rough pinion every day...

Killer of Life and Art, assassin dark,
You'll never banish from my memory
The one who was my joy and majesty!

CHARLES BAUDELAIRE

Le Balcon

Mère des souvenirs, maîtresse des maîtresses,
 Ô toi, tous mes plaisirs! ô toi, tous mes devoirs!
Tu te rappelleras la beauté des caresses,
La douceur du foyer et le charme des soirs,
Mère des souvenirs, maîtresse des maîtresses!

Les soirs illuminés par l'ardeur du charbon,
Et les soirs au balcon, voilés de vapeurs roses.
Que ton sein m'était doux! que ton cœur m'était bon!
Nous avons dit souvent d'impérissables choses
Les soirs illuminés par l'ardeur du charbon.

Que les soleils sont beaux dans les chaudes soirées!
Que l'espace est profond! que le cœur est puissant!
En me penchant vers toi, reine des adorées,
Je croyais respirer le parfum de ton sang.
Que les soleils sont beaux dans les chaudes soirées!

La nuit s'épaississait ainsi qu'une cloison,
Et mes yeux dans le noir devinaient tes prunelles,
Et je buvais ton souffle, ô douceur! ô poison!
Et tes pieds s'endormaient dans mes mains fraternelles.
La nuit s'épaississait ainsi qu'une cloison.

Je sais l'art d'évoquer les minutes heureuses,
Et revis mon passé blotti dans tes genoux.
Car à quoi bon chercher tes beautés langoureuses
Ailleurs qu'en ton cher corps et qu'en ton cœur si doux?
Je sais l'art d'évoquer les minutes heureuses!

Ces serments, ces parfums, ces baisers infinis,
Renaîtront-ils d'un gouffre interdit à nos sondes,
Comme montent au ciel les soleils rajeunis
Après s'être lavés au fond des mers profondes?
— Ô serments! ô parfums! ô baisers infinis!

CHARLES BAUDELAIRE

The Balcony

Mother of memories, mistress of mistresses,
O you my every bliss, O you my every duty,
You will recall the joy of our profound caresses,
The comfort of the hearth, the evening's tranquil beauty,
Mother of memories, mistress of mistresses!

The evenings by the fire, lit by the burning coal,
And on the balcony, veiled in a rosy hue,
The softness of your breast, the sweetness of your soul!
We said so many things that were forever true,
The evenings by the fire, lit by the burning coal!

How beautiful the sunlight on a summer's night!
How deep the vault of heaven! How strong the beating heart!
Holding you close to me, O queen of my delight,
It seemed your very blood did its sweet scent impart.
How beautiful the sunlight on a summer's night!

The wall of darkness thickened, shutting out the light,
And in the gloom my eyes sought your eyes longingly,
And I imbibed your breath, O poisonous delight!
And in my loving hands your feet slept peacefully.
The wall of darkness thickened, shutting out the light.

The recollection of sweet moments is an art
That lets me live again those hours of happiness.
Why should I seek elsewhere than in your loving heart,
And in your gracious form, the joys of languidness?
The recollection of sweet moments is an art!

Those vows, those fragrant scents, those kisses without end,
Can they be born again from gulfs we cannot sound,
Just as the endless seas back to the heavens send
Rejuvenated suns that from their depths rebound?
— O vows! O fragrant scents! O kisses without end!

CHARLES BAUDELAIRE

Le Vin des amants

Aujourd'hui l'espace est splendide!
Sans mors, sans éperons, sans bride,
Partons à cheval sur le vin
Pour un ciel féerique et divin!

Comme deux anges que torture
Une implacable calenture,
Dans le bleu cristal du matin
Suivons le mirage lointain!

Mollement balancés sur l'aile
Du tourbillon intelligent,
Dans un délire parallèle,

Ma sœur, côte à côte nageant,
Nous fuirons sans repos ni trêves
Vers le paradis de mes rêves!

CHARLES BAUDELAIRE

The Lovers' Wine

How splendid is the world today!
Without bit or spur, lets away
Upon our mounts of heady wine
To heavens magic and divine!

Like two angels tormented by
An ardent flame that will not die,
In the bright morning's crystal blue
Let us the far mirage pursue.

Riding and rocking languidly
On an all-knowing, swirling tide,
In a parallel ecstasy,

My sister, floating side by side,
We'll follow these exotic streams
To the nirvana of my dreams!

CHARLES BAUDELAIRE

La Mort des amants

Nous aurons des lits pleins d'odeurs légères,
Des divans profonds comme des tombeaux,
Et d'étranges fleurs sur des étagères,
Ecloses pour nous sous des cieux plus beaux.

Usant à l'envi leurs chaleurs dernières,
Nos deux cœurs seront deux vastes flambeaux,
Qui réfléchiront leurs doubles lumières
Dans nos deux esprits, ces miroirs jumeaux.

Un soir fait de rose et de bleu mystique,
Nous échangerons un éclair unique,
Comme un long sanglot, tout chargé d'adieux;

Et plus tard un Ange, entr'ouvrant les portes,
Viendra ranimer, fidèle et joyeux,
Les miroirs ternis et les flammes mortes.

CHARLES BAUDELAIRE

The Lovers' Death

We shall have beds imbued with subtle scents,
And ottomans as deep as any tomb,
And flow'rs of mystic fragrance redolent
That under fairer skies for us will bloom.

Burning ever more ardent and more bright,
Our hearts will shine like beacons from above,
Each sending forth its pure reflected light
To the twin mirrors of our endless love.

One evening made of rose and mystic blue,
We shall exchange an ultimate adieu,
A last scintilla of this earthly life;

And later an Angelic form will pass,
To faithfully and joyously revive
The dormant embers and the tarnished glass.

MATTHEW ARNOLD (1822 1888)

Longing

Come to me in my dreams, and then
By day I shall be well again.
For then the night will more than pay
The hopeless longing of the day.

Come, as thou cam'st a thousand times,
A messenger from radiant climes,
And smile on thy new world, and be
As kind to others as to me.

Or, as thou never cam'st in sooth,
Come now, and let me dream it truth.
And part my hair, and kiss my brow,
And say My love! why sufferest thou?

Come to me in my dreams, and then
By day I shall be well again.
For then the night will more than pay
The hopeless longing of the day.

STEPHEN FOSTER (1826 –1864)

Beautiful dreamer, wake unto me ...

Beautiful dreamer, wake unto me,
Starlight and dewdrops are waiting for thee;
Sounds of the rude world heard in the day,
Lull'd by the moonlight have all pass'd a way!

Beautiful dreamer, queen of my song,
List while I woo thee with soft melody;
Gone are the cares of life's busy throng, —
Beautiful dreamer, awake unto me!

Beautiful dreamer, out on the sea
Mermaids are chaunting the wild lorelie;
Over the streamlet vapors are borne,
Waiting to fade at the bright coming morn.

Beautiful dreamer, beam on my heart,
E'en as the morn on the streamlet and sea;
Then will all clouds of sorrow depart, —
Beautiful dreamer, awake unto me!

STEPHEN FOSTER

I dream of Jeanie with the light brown hair ...

I dream of Jeanie with the light brown hair,
Borne, like a vapor on the summer air;
I see her playing where the bright streams play,
Happy as the daisies that dance on her way.
Many were the wild notes her merry voice would pour.
Many were the blithe birds that warbled them o'er:
Oh, I dream of Jeanie with the light brown hair,
Floating, like a vapor, on the soft summer air.

I long for Jeanie with a day-dawn smile,
Radiant in gladness, warm with winning guile;
I hear her melodies, like joys gone by,
Sighing round my heart over the fond hopes that die:
Sighing like the night wind and sobbing like the rain,
Wailing for the lost one that comes not again:
Oh, I long for Jeanie, and my heart bows low,
Never more to find her where the bright waters flow.

I sigh for Jeanie, but her light form strayed
Far from the fond hearts round her native glade;
Her smiles have vanished and her sweet songs flown,
Flitting like the dreams that have cheered us and gone.
Now the nodding wild flowers may wither on the shore
While her gentle fingers will cull them no more:
Oh, I sigh for Jeanie with the light brown hair,
Floating, like a vapor, on the soft summer air.

CHRISTINA ROSSETTI (1830 - 1894)

Remember

Remember me when I am gone away,
Gone far away into the silent land;
When you can no more hold me by the hand,
Nor I half turn to go yet turning stay.
Remember me when no more day by day
You tell me of our future that you plann'd:
Only remember me; you understand
It will be late to counsel then or pray.
Yet if you should forget me for a while
And afterwards remember, do not grieve:
For if the darkness and corruption leave
A vestige of the thoughts that once I had,
Better by far you should forget and smile
Than that you should remember and be sad.

CHRISTINA ROSSETTI

I loved you first...

I loved you first: but afterwards your love
Outsoaring mine, sang such a loftier song
As drowned the friendly cooings of my dove.
Which owes the other most? my love was long,
And yours one moment seemed to wax more strong;
I loved and guessed at you, you construed me
And loved me for what might or might not be –
Nay, weights and measures do us both a wrong.
For verily love knows not 'mine' or 'thine;'
With separate 'I' and 'thou' free love has done,
For one is both and both are one in love:
Rich love knows nought of 'thine that is not mine;'
Both have the strength and both the length thereof,
Both of us, of the love which makes us one.

CHRISTINA ROSSETTI

The First Day

I wish I could remember the first day,
First hour, first moment of your meeting me;
If bright or dim the season it might be;
Summer or winter for aught I can say.
So, unrecorded did it slip away,
So blind was i to see and to forsee,
So dull to mark the budding of my tree
That would not blossom, yet, for many a May.
If only I could recollect it! Such
A day of days! I let it come and go
As traceless as a thaw of bygone snow.
It seemed to mean so little, meant so much!
If only now I could recall that touch,
First touch of hand in hand! - Did one but know!

CHRISTINA ROSSETTI

Somewhere or other...

Somewhere or other there must surely be
The face not seen, the voice not heard,
The heart that not yet — never yet — ah me!
Made answer to my word.

Somewhere or other, may be near or far;
Past land and sea, clean out of sight;
Beyond the wandering moon, beyond the star
That tracks her night by night.

Somewhere or other, may be far or near;
With just a wall, a hedge, between;
With just the last leaves of the dying year
Fallen on a turf grown green.

CHRISTINA ROSSETTI

Echo

Come to me in the silence of the night;
Come in the sparkling silence of a dream;
Come with soft rounded cheeks and eyes as bright
As sunlight on a stream;
Come back in tears,
O memory, hope, love of finished years.

O dream how sweet, too sweet, too bitter sweet,
Whose wakening should have been in Paradise,
Where souls brimfull of love abide and meet;
Where thirsting longing eyes
Watch the slow door
That opening, letting in, lets out no more.

Yet come to me in dreams, that I may live
My very life again though cold in death:
Come back to me in dreams, that I may give
Pulse for pulse, breath for breath:
Speak low, lean low,
As long ago, my love, how long ago.

EMILY DICKINSON (1830 – 1886)

A charm invests a face...

A charm invests a face
Imperfectly beheld.
The lady dare not lift her veil
For fear it be dispelled.

But peers beyond her mesh,
And wishes, and denies,
Lest interview annul a want
That image satisfies.

EMILY DICKINSON

For each ecstatic instant...

For each ecstatic instant
We must an anguish pay.
In keen and quivering ratio
To the ecstasy.

For each beloved hour
Sharp pittances of years,
Bitter contested farthings
And coffers heaped with tears.

EMILY DICKINSON

You left me, sweet...

You left me, sweet, two legacies, -
A legacy of love
A Heavenly Father would content,
Had He the offer of;

You left me boundaries of pain
Capacious as the sea,
Between eternity and time,
Your consciousness and me.

EMILY DICKINSON

If you were coming in the fall…

If you were coming in the fall
I'd brush the summer by
With half a smile and half a spurn
As housewives do a fly.

If I could see you in a year
I'd wind the months in balls
And put them into separate drawers
Until their time befalls.

If only centuries delayed
I'd count them on my hand
Subtracting 'till my fingers dropped
Into Van Diemen's land

If certain when this life was out
That yours and mine should be
I'd toss life yonder like a rind
And taste eternity.

But now all ignorant of length,
Of times uncertain wing,
It goads me like the goblin bee
That will not state its sting!

WILLIAM MORRIS (1834 – 1896)

Love is enough…

Love is enough: though the World be a-waning,
And the woods have no voice but the voice of complaining,
Though the sky be too dark for dim eyes to discover
The gold-cups and daisies fair blooming thereunder,
Though the hills be held shadows, and the sea a dark wonder
And this day draw a veil over all deeds pass'd over,
Yet their hands shall not tremble, their feet shall not falter;
The void shall not weary, the fear shall not alter
These lips and these eyes of the loved and the lover.

ALFRED AUSTIN (1835 – 1913)

Love's Trinity

Soul, heart, and body, we thus singly name,
Are not in love divisible and distinct,
But each with each inseparably link'd.
One is not honour, and the other shame,
But burn as closely fused as fuel, heat, and flame.

They do not love who give the body and keep
The heart ungiven; nor they who yield the soul,
And guard the body. Love doth give the whole;
Its range being high as heaven, as ocean deep,
Wide as the realms of air or planet's curving sweep.

HENRI CAZALIS (1840 – 1909)

Sérénade florentine

Étoile dont la beauté luit
Comme un diamant dans la nuit,
Regarde vers ma bien-aimée
Dont la paupière s'est fermée.

Et fais descendre sur ses yeux
La bénédiction des cieux.
Elle s'endort... Par la fenêtre
En sa chambre heureuse pénètre;

Sur sa blancheur, comme un baiser,
Viens jusqu'à l'aube te poser
Et que sa pensée, alors, rêve
D'un astre d'amour qui se lève!

HENRI CAZALIS (1840 – 1909)

Florentine Serenade

O star, whose pure transparent light
Shines like a diamond in the night,
Look down upon my love's repose
As her eyes now in slumber close.

Bestow on her beloved eyes
The benediction of the skies.
She sleeps now; let her room tonight
Be bathed in your translucent light.

Upon her whiteness, like a kiss,
Alight till dawn disturbs her bliss,
And may she dream that up above
There rose a nascent star of love.

HENRI CAZALIS

Dans ton cœur dort un clair de lune...

Dans ton cœur dort un clair de lune,
Un doux clair de lune d'été,
Et pour fuir la vie importune,
Je me noierai dans ta clarté.

J'oublierai les douleurs passées,
Mon amour, quand tu berceras
Mon triste cœur et mes pensées
Dans le calme aimant de tes bras.

Tu prendras ma tête malade,
Oh! Quelquefois, sur tes genoux,
Et lui diras une ballade
Qui semblera parler de nous;

Et dans tes yeux pleins de tristesse,
Dans tes yeux alors je boirai
Tant de baisers et de tendresses
Que peut-être je guérirai.

HENRI CAZALIS

The Antidote

In your heart sleeps a pale moonlight,
A gentle summer's evening,
And from life's turmoil taking flight
I shall immerse myself therein.

Past sorrows from my soul shall fly,
My darling, when your arms enlace
My troubled thoughts and aching heart
Within the calm of your embrace.

You'll cool the fever of my brow
With soft caresses from above,
And you will sing a ballad song
That tells the story of our love;

And in the haven of your eyes,
Sad eyes that understand my pain,
I shall imbibe such tenderness
That I shall be made well again.

THOMAS HARDY (1840 – 1928)

Neutral Tones

We stood by a pond that winter day,
And the sun was white, as though chidden of God,
And a few leaves lay on the starving sod;
– They had fallen from an ash, and were grey.

Your eyes on me were as eyes that rove
Over tedious riddles of years ago;
And some words played between us to and fro
On which lost the more by our love.

The smile on your mouth was the deadest thing
Alive enough to have strength to die;
And a grin of bitterness swept thereby
Like an ominous bird a-wing….

Since then, keen lessons that love deceives,
And wrings with wrong, have shaped to me
Your face, and the God curst sun, and a tree,
And a pond edged with greyish leaves.

THOMAS HARDY

The Voice

Woman much missed, how you call to me, call to me,
Saying that now you are not as you were
When you had changed from the one who was all to me,
But as at first, when our day was fair.
Can it be you that I hear? Let me view you, then,
Standing as when I drew near to the town
Where you would wait for me: yes, as I knew you then,
Even to the original air-blue gown!

Or is it only the breeze in its listlessness
Travelling across the wet mead to me here,
You being ever dissolved to wan wistlessness,
Heard no more again far or near?

Thus I; faltering forward,
Leaves around me falling,
Wind oozing thin through the thorn from norward,
And the woman calling.

ROBERT SEYMOUR BRIDGES (1844—1930)

My delight and thy delight...

My delight and thy delight
Walking, like two angels white,
In the gardens of the night:

My desire and thy desire
Twining to a tongue of fire,
Leaping live, and laughing higher:

Thro' the everlasting strife
In the mystery of life.

Love, from whom the world begun,
Hath the secret of the sun.

Love can tell, and love alone,
Whence the million stars were strewn,
Why each atom knows its own,
How, in spite of woe and death,
Gay is life, and sweet is breath:

This he taught us, this we knew,
Happy in his science true,
Hand in hand as we stood
'Neath the shadows of the wood,
Heart to heart as we lay
In the dawning of the day.

ROBERT SEYMOUR BRIDGES

So sweet love seemed that April morn...

So sweet love seemed that April morn,
When first we kissed beside the thorn,
So strangely sweet, it was not strange
We thought that love could never change.

But I can tell--let truth be told--
That love will change in growing old;
Though day by day is naught to see,
So delicate his motions be.

And in the end 'twill come to pass
Quite to forget what once he was,
Nor even in fancy to recall
The pleasure that was all in all.

His little spring, that sweet we found,
So deep in summer floods is drowned,
I wonder, bathed in joy complete,
How love so young could be so sweet.

ROBERT SEYMOUR BRIDGES

I will not let thee go

I will not let thee go.
Ends all our month-long love in this?
Can it be summed up so,
Quit in a single kiss?
I will not let thee go.

I will not let thee go.
If thy words' breath could scare thy deeds,
As the soft south can blow
And toss the feathered seeds,
Then might I let thee go.

I will not let thee go.
Had not the great sun seen, I might;
Or were he reckoned slow
To bring the false to light,
Then might I let thee go.

I will not let thee go.
The stars that crowd the summer skies
Have watched us so below
With all their million eyes,
I dare not let thee go.

I will not let thee go.
Have we chid the changeful moon,
Now rising late, and now
Because she set too soon,
And shall I let thee go?

ROBERT SEYMOUR BRIDGES

I will not let thee go.
Have not the young flowers been content,
Plucked ere their buds could blow,
To seal our sacrament?
I cannot let thee go.

I will not let thee go.
I hold thee by too many bands:
Thou sayest farewell, and lo!
I have thee by the hands,
And will not let thee go.

PAUL VERLAINE (1844 –1896)

Mon Rêve Familier

Je fais souvent ce rêve étrange et pénétrant
D'une femme inconnue, et que j'aime, et qui m'aime,
Et qui n'est, chaque fois, ni tout à fait la même,
Ni tout à fait une autre, et m'aime, et me comprend.

Car elle me comprend, et mon cœur, transparent
Pour elle seule hélas cesse d'être un problème
Pour elle seule, et les moiteurs de mon front blême
Elle seule les sait rafraîchir, en pleurant.

Est-elle brune, blonde ou rousse? je l'ignore...
Son nom? je me souviens qu'il est doux et sonore,
Comme ceux des aimés que la Vie exila;

Son regard est pareil au regard des statues
Et, pour sa voix, lointaine, et calme et grave, elle a
L'inflexion des voix chères qui se sont tues.

PAUL VERLAINE (1844 –1896)

My Familiar Dream

I often have this strange and penetrating dream
About a woman, whom I love and who loves me,
And who, each time I dream, is never quite the same,
Yet never quite another; and strangely, it would seem

She understands my cares, my sorrows and my fears.
She looks into my soul, sees what afflicts me now,
So that she can console me, cool my fevered brow,
And wash away my pain and sorrow with her tears.

Is her hair auburn, dark, or fair? - I do not know.
Her name? - As I recall, its gentle accents flow
In names of those I loved, now exiled from this life.

Her eyes are reminiscent of a statue's mystic gaze.
Her voice, mellifluous and gentle, brings to mind
A voice I knew so well – a voice from bygone days.

PAUL VERLAINE

Chanson d'Automne

Les sanglots longs
Des violons
De l'automne
Blessent mon cœur
D'une langueur
Monotone.

Tout suffocant
Et blême, quand
Sonne l'heure,
Je me souviens
Des jours anciens
Et je pleure.

Et je m'en vais
Au vent mauvais
Qui m'emporte
Deçà, delà,
Pareil à la
Feuille morte.

PAUL VERLAINE

Autumn Song

The long lament
Of autumn's
Symphony
Assails my heart
With deep
Melancholy.

Tearful and pale
When tolls the
Vesper bell,
I call to mind
Past time
When Love was well.

O how the chill wind
Now my heart
Bereaves,
Blown here and there,
Just like the
Falling leaves.

OSCAR WILDE (1854 –1900)

To My Wife

I can write no stately poem
As a prelude to my lay;
From a poet to a poem
I would dare to say.
For if of these fallen petals
One to you seem fair,
Love will waft it till it settles
On your hair.
And when wind and winter harden
All the loveless land,
It will whisper of the garden,
You will understand.

And there is nothing left to do
But to kiss once again, and part,
Nay, there is nothing we should rue,
I have my beauty,-you your Art,
Nay, do not start,
One world was not enough for two
Like me and you.

EDITH NESBITT (1858 - 1924)

A Tragedy

Among his books he sits all day
To think and read and write;
He does not smell the new-mown hay,
The roses red and white.

I walk among them all alone,
His silly, stupid wife;
The world seems tasteless, dead and done —
An empty thing is life.

At night his window casts a square
Of light upon the lawn;
I sometimes walk and watch it there
Until the chill of dawn.

I have no brain to understand
The books he loves to read;
I only have a heart and hand
He does not seem to need.

He calls me "Child" — lays on my hair
Thin fingers, cold and mild;
Oh! God of Love, who answers prayer,
I wish I were a child!

And no one sees and no one knows
(He least would know or see),
That ere Love gathers next year's rose
Death will have gathered me.

A. E. HOUSMAN (1859 – 1936)

When the lad for longing sighs...

When the lad for longing sighs,
Mute and dull of cheer and pale,
If at death's own door he lies,
Maiden, you can heal his ail.

Lovers' ills are all to buy:
The wan look, the hollow tone,
The hung head, the sunken eye,
You can have them for your own.

Buy them, buy them: even and morn
Lovers' ills are all to sell,
Then you can lie down forlorn;
But the lover will be well.

A. E. HOUSMAN

Oh, when I was in love with you...

Oh, when I was in love with you
Then I was clean and brave,
And miles around the wonder grew
How well did I behave.

And now the fancy passes by
And nothing will remain,
And miles around they'll say that I
Am quite myself again.

A. E. HOUSMAN

When I was one-and-twenty…

When I was one-and-twenty
I heard a wise man say,
"Give crowns and pounds and guineas
But not your heart away;
Give pearls away and rubies
But keep your fancy free."
But I was one-and-twenty,
No use to talk to me.

When I was one-and-twenty
I heard him say again,
"The heart out of the bosom
Was never given in vain;
'Tis paid with sighs a plenty
And sold for endless rue."
And I am two-and-twenty,
And oh, 'tis true, 'tis true.

SIR ARTHUR SOMERVELL (1863 –1937)

Silent Worship

Did you not hear my Lady
Go down the garden singing?
Blackbird and thrush were silent
To hear the alleys ringing.

Oh, saw you not my Lady
Out in the garden there,
Shaming the rose and lily,
For she is twice as fair.

Though I am nothing to her,
Though she must rarely look at me,
And though I could never woo her,
I love her till I die.

Surely you heard my Lady
Go down the garden singing,
Silencing all the songbirds
And setting the alleys ringing...

But surely you saw my Lady
Out in the garden there,
Rivalling the glittering sunshine
With a glory of golden hair.

WILLIAM BUTLER YEATS (1865 – 1939)

When you are old and grey…

When you are old and grey and full of sleep,
And, nodding by the fire, take down this book,
And slowly read, and dream of the soft look
Your eyes had once, and of their shadows deep.

How many loved your moments of glad grace
And loved your beauty with love false or true,
But one man loved the pilgrim soul in you,
And loved the sorrows of your changing face.

And bending down beside the glowing bars,
Murmur, a little sadly, how Love fled
And paced upon the mountain overhead
And hid his face amid a crowd of stars.

cf. *Sonnet for Helen*, page 17

WILLIAM BUTLER YEATS

Down by the Salley Gardens...

Down by the Salley Gardens
My love and I did meet;
She passed the Salley Gardens
With little snow-white feet.
She bid me take love easy,
As the leaves grow on the tree;
But I, being young and foolish,
With her would not agree.

In a field by the river
My love and I did stand,
And on my leaning shoulder
She laid her snow-white hand.
She bid me take life easy,
As the grass grows on the weirs;
But I was young and foolish,
And now am full of tears.

GUILLAUME APOLLINAIRE (1880 – 1918)

Le Pont Mirabeau

Sous le pont Mirabeau coule la Seine
Et nos amours
Faut-il qu'il m'en souvienne
La joie venait toujours après la peine

Vienne la nuit sonne l'heure
Les jours s'en vont je demeure

Les mains dans les mains restons face à face
Tandis que sous
Le pont de nos bras passe
Des éternels regards l'onde si lasse

Vienne la nuit sonne l'heure
Les jours s'en vont je demeure

L'amour s'en va comme cette eau courante
L'amour s'en va
Comme la vie est lente
Et comme l'Espérance est violente

Vienne la nuit sonne l'heure
Les jours s'en vont je demeure

Passent les jours et passent les semaines
Ni temps passé
Ni les amours reviennent
Sous le pont Mirabeau coule la Seine

Vienne la nuit sonne l'heure
Les jours s'en vont je demeure

GUILLAUME APOLLINAIRE (1880 – 1918)

The Mirabeau Bridge

Beneath the Mirabeau Bridge flows the Seine
And our amours
Must I remember them
The joy would always come after the pain

Toll the midnight bell again
Days depart I remain

Hands entwined we idly passed our days
While underneath
The arms of our embrace
Flowed waters weary of our endless gaze

Toll the midnight bell again
Days depart I remain

Love flows away just as these waters flow
Love flows away
O how this life is slow
And how our hopes conspire to lay us low

Toll the midnight bell again
Days depart I remain

The days pass by in time's relentless flow
Neither past time
Nor love can ever now
Return beneath the Bridge of Mirabeau

Toll the midnight bell again
Days depart I remain

SARA TEASDALE (1884—1933)

The Kiss

I hoped that he would love me,
And he has kissed my mouth,
But I am like a stricken bird
That cannot reach the south.

For though I know he loves me,
To-night my heart is sad;
His kiss was not so wonderful
As all the dreams I had.

SARA TEASDALE

I am not yours…

I am not yours, not lost in you,
Not lost, although I long to be
Lost as a candle lit at noon,
Lost as a snowflake in the sea.

You love me, and I find you still
A spirit beautiful and bright,
Yet I am I, who long to be
Lost as a light is lost in light.

Oh plunge me deep in love - put out
My senses, leave me deaf and blind,
Swept by the tempest of your love,
A taper in a rushing wind.

SARA TEASDALE

Alone

I am alone, in spite of love,
In spite of all I take and give —
In spite of all your tenderness,
Sometimes I am not glad to live.

I am alone, as though I stood
On the highest peak of the tired gray world,
About me only swirling snow,
Above me, endless space unfurled;

With earth hidden and heaven hidden,
And only my own spirit's pride
To keep me from the peace of those
Who are not lonely, having died.

RUPERT BROOKE (1887 - 1915)

Love

Love is a breach in the walls, a broken gate,
Where that comes in that shall not go again;
Love sells the proud heart's citadel to Fate.
They have known shame, who love unloved. Even then,
When two mouths, thirsty each for each, find slaking,
And agony's forgot, and hushed the crying
Of credulous hearts, in heaven -- such are but taking
Their own poor dreams within their arms, and lying
Each in his lonely night, each with a ghost.
Some share that night. But they know love grows colder,
Grows false and dull, that was sweet lies at most.
Astonishment is no more in hand or shoulder,
But darkens, and dies out from kiss to kiss.
All this is love; and all love is but this.

RUPERT BROOKE

Beauty and Beauty

When Beauty and Beauty meet
All naked, fair to fair,
The earth is crying-sweet,
And scattering-bright the air,
Eddying, dizzying, closing round,
With soft and drunken laughter;
Veiling all that may befall
After -- after --

Where Beauty and Beauty met,
Earth's still a-tremble there,
And winds are scented yet,
And memory-soft the air,
Bosoming, folding glints of light,
And shreds of shadowy laughter;
Not the tears that fill the years
After -- after –

EDITOR'S NOTE

I have included the original French and German texts in order to illustrate how a poem in another language can sometimes be freely adapted into English, or even simply used as inspiration for a new poem. W. B. Yeats took inspiration for his famous poem *When you are old and grey* from Ronsard's *Sonnet pour Hélène*, but the two poems differ sufficiently for Yeats's poem to become a new poem, whereas my version, *Sonnet for Helen,* is much closer to the original French.

Looking at two more poems in this anthology, *Welcome and Farewell* is a near adaptation of Goethe's *Willkommen und Abschied*, whereas *Would You Were Here!*, also based on a poem by Goethe, is sufficiently different from the original to become a new poem.

The translations and adaptations of poems by Ronsard, Goethe, Schober, Heine, Rellstab, Hugo, Arvers, Cazalis, Verlaine and Apollinaire are all previously unpublished. The Baudelaire poems were first published in the 2016 dual language edition of *Les Fleurs du Mal: The Flowers of Evil*, ISBN 978-1533212436.

John E. Tidball, March 2021

Index of Poets

Apollinaire, Guillaume   162
Arnold, Matthew   126
Arvers, Félix   88
Austin, Alfred   139
Baudelaire, Charles   104
Blake, William   50
Bradstreet, Anne   38
Breton, Nicholas   18
Bridges, Robert Seymour   146
Brooke, Rupert   167
Browning, Elizabeth Barrett   86
Browning, Robert   99
Burns, Robert   52
Byron, George Gordon   60
Campion, Thomas   28
Cazalis, Henri   140
Clare, John   65
Coleridge, Samuel Taylor   57
Dickinson, Emily   134
Drayton, Michael   22
Dryden, John   40
Eliot, George   101
Fletcher, John   32
Ford, Thomas   33
Foster, Stephen   127
Goethe, Johann Wolfgang von   46
Hardy, Thomas   144
Heine, Heinrich   72
Herbert, George   36
Herrick, Robert   34
Hood, Thomas   80
Housman, A. E.   156
Hugo, Victor   84
Johnson, Samuel   42
Jonson, Ben   29
Keats, John   67
Kingsley, Charles   102
Lovelace, Richard   39
Marlowe, Christopher   26
Moore, Thomas   59

Morris, William 138
Nesbitt, Edith 155
Opie, Amelia 54
Poe, Edgar Allan 96
Rellstab, Ludwig 82
Ronsard, Pierre de 14
Rossetti, Christina 129
Schober, Franz von 70
Shakespeare, William 23
Shelley, Percy Bysshe 63
Sidney, Sir Philip 21
Somervell, Sir Arthur 159
Southey, Robert 58
Spenser, Edmund 19
Suckling, Sir John 37
Teasdale, Sara 164
Tennyson, Alfred 90
Verlaine, Paul 150
Wilbye, John 31
Wilde, Oscar 154
Wilmot, John 41
Yeats, William Butler 160

Index of Titles and First Lines

À Cassandre   14
A charm invests a face... 134
A Dream Within a Dream   96
A Farewell   102
A Red, Red Rose   52
A Tragedy   155
À une passante   104
All of Her   117
Alone   166
Am Bach im Frühling   70
Amaryllis   28
Annabel Lee   97
Autumn Song   153
Beautiful dreamer, wake unto me ... 127
Beauty and Beauty
Birds in the high hall garden... 92
Break, break, break... 90
Bright Star   67
By the Brook in Springtime   71
Come into the garden, Maud... 93
Dans ton cœur dort un clair de lune... 142
Demain, dès l'aube... 84
Die Lotosblume   72
Down by the Salley Gardens... 161
Echo   133
Ein Jüngling liebt ein Mädchen... 76
Evening Ode   42
Fair and True   18
First Love   65
Florentine Serenade   141
For each ecstatic instant... 135
Go not, happy day... 91
Go, Valentine... 58
Hidden Flame   40
How do I love thee? Let me count the ways... 87
How Can I Forget?   66
Hymn   115
Hymne...114
I am not yours... 165

175

I dream of Jeanie with the light brown hair ... 128
I loved you first... 130
I prithee send me back my heart... 37
I will not let thee go... 148
Ice and Fire   19
If thou must love me, let it be for nought... 86
If you were coming in the fall... 137
Invitation to a Journey   111
L'Invitation au voyage   110
La Mort des amants   124
Le Balcon   120
Le Jet d'eau   106
Le Pont Mirabeau   162
Le Portrait   118
Le Sonnet de Félix Arvers   78
Le Vin des amants   122
Let me not to the marriage of true minds... 24
Life in a Love   100
Longing   126
Lorelei (German)   78
Lorelei (English)   79
Love (Rupert Brooke)   167
Love (George Herbert)   36
Love's Philosophy   64
Love's Trinity   139
Love and Life   41
Love is enough   138
Love not me for comely grace... 31
Mon âme a son secret; ma vie a sa mystère... 88
Mon rêve familier   150
My delight and thy delight... 146
My Familiar Dream   151
My love is as a fever, longing still... 25
My Pretty Rose Tree   51
My soul conceals a secret, my life a mystery... 89
My true love hath my heart... 21
Nähe des Geliebten   46
Neutral Tones   144
Now   99
Ode to Cassandre   15

176

Oh, when I was in love with you… 157
One day I wrote her name… 20
Remember   129
Ruth…81
Saphire sind die Augen dein… 74
Secret Love   54
Serenade   83
Sérénade florentine   140
Shall I compare thee to a summer's day?   23
She is far from the land… 59
She walks in beauty… 61
Silent Worship   159
Since there's no help… 22
So sweet love seemed that April morn… 147
So we'll go no more a-roving… 60
Somewhere or other there must surely be… 132
Song to Celia —I 29
Song to Celia — II 30
Sonnet 18 (Shakespeare)   23
Sonnet 116 (Shakespeare)   24
Sonnet 147 (Shakespeare)   25
Sonnet 14 (Elizabeth Barrett Browning)   86
Sonnet 43 (Elizabeth Barrett Browning)   87
Sonnet pour Hélène   16
Sonnet for Helen   17
Ständchen   82
Sweet Disorder   35
Sweet evenings come and go, love… 101
Summer   44
Take, oh, take those lips away… 32
Tell me not, Sweet… 39
The Antidote   143
The Balcony   120
The Coveted Jewels   75
The First Day   131
The Fountain   107
The Garden of Love   50
The Journey   85
The Kiss   164
The Lovers' Death   125

The Lovers' Wine   123
The Lotus Flower   72
The Mirabeau Bridge   163
The Parting Kiss   53
The Passionate Shepherd to his Love   26
The Portrait   119
The Presence of Love   57
The Sonnet of Félix Arvers   79
The Voice   145
The Winter's Walk   43
There is a lady sweet and kind… 33
Time of Roses   80
To a Passer-By   105
To Fanny Brawne   68
To Jane   63
To My Dear and Loving Husband   38
To My Wife   154
To Stella   45
To Virgins, to make much of Time   34
Tout entière   116
Unrequited Love   77
Welcome and Farewell   49
When I was one-and-twenty… 158
When the lad for longing sighs… 156
When we two parted… 62
When you are old and grey… 160
Who Ever Loved, That Loved Not at First Sight?   27
Willkommen und Abschied   48
Would You Were Here!   47
You left me, sweet… 136
You say you love: but with a voice …
Young and Old   103

Printed in Great Britain
by Amazon